The
Christian
Encounters

CRIME IN AMERICAN SOCIETY

Richard D. Knudten

//

N.C. B.C.

Concordia Publishing House
Saint Louis   London

Concordia Publishing House, St. Louis, Missouri
Concordia Publishing House Ltd., London, E. C. 1
© 1969 Concordia Publishing House
Library of Congress Catalog Card No. 69-17597

MANUFACTURED IN THE UNITED STATES OF AMERICA

Contents

Preface

Charges of Supreme Court incompetence, coddling of criminals, and demands for greater police control dominate the news after the riots and violence of recent years. Some charges are true; others are out of touch with reality. Some citizens store guns; others burn buildings. Some cry for gun control; others call for absolute individual freedom. The cries are loud; the responses weak. Several officials suggest the preservation of freedom by suppression of the rights of freedom. Others argue in protest that only a reconstruction of society can reestablish public justice and eliminate private privilege. The ominous findings of the Kerner Report concerning the problems of "white racism," antagonism between Negroes and police, riots' causes, and suggested solutions do little to establish public confidence in the stability of modern society.

Christians are not above these influences. At times they may reflect prevailing attitudes of culture more than the views of Christian faith. Church members, too, may look for simple solutions of complex problems in times of crisis. They may join those who suggest that the publication of names of delinquents will eliminate their delinquency, that harsher punishments will lessen crime, and that enforced morality will enhance public life. Threat of loss and danger to life may lead to despair instead of hope and to hate in place of love. Reasoning that murder occurs with greater frequency, at least as reported in the newspapers, citizens may fail to perceive that the increase is proportionately less than the population increase. They may not realize that more crime can be expected as a consequence of population growth. Although they call for greater crime control, citizens tend to excuse war, which causes more widespread destruction of life and property than delinquency and crime. The quest for security in an age of change makes people suspicious of those who wander away from the values of the rural past when in search of the urban future. Personal fears, racial prejudice, ideological commitment and—in some instances—a deficient Christian perspective obstruct understanding of the real situation and block effective action toward the improvement of social conditions.

These are not easy times. They demand patience and intelligence for gaining the accurate information supplied by research and for understanding the Biblical view of man according to the Christian faith. Our day calls for men of vision to interpret Christian truth to those whose lives are shattered. Christians use the knowledge of sociology and other social sciences to understand human conditions and problems; their concern for people is motivated by the love of Jesus Christ, and their goal is to serve all men as neighbors. They believe and proclaim the Gospel that Christ came to make all men whole, by assuming their guilt in His life and death, and to give them new life by His rising from death. This love of Christ moves Christians to regard every single human life as sacred even in this period of extensive social change.

Crime in American Society presents some of the challenges, issues, and facts concerning delinquency and crime. We discuss some of the realities based on the findings of sociological and criminological studies. We describe various theories regarding the origins of criminality. The problems of law enforcement and individual and group rights are discussed from several angles. We examine judicial and penal systems and consider proposals for improvement and reform. These are concerns of the Christian who serves as God's agent in the world to work for good government, justice, care of the needy, and rehabilitation of criminals. In the public domain the Christian works and lives in the area of God's law. He does what he can to improve society and the social conditions of individuals. As one who lives under the Gospel in a forgiven relationship with God, the Christian believes the underlying cause of criminality is man's alienation from God. The Christian's concern is especially for the personal transformation and renewal of man by the Spirit of God in a relationship of faith in the reconciliation with God accomplished by Jesus Christ. A deep concern for justice and for the spiritual renewal of men motivates the Christian in his encounter with crime in American society.

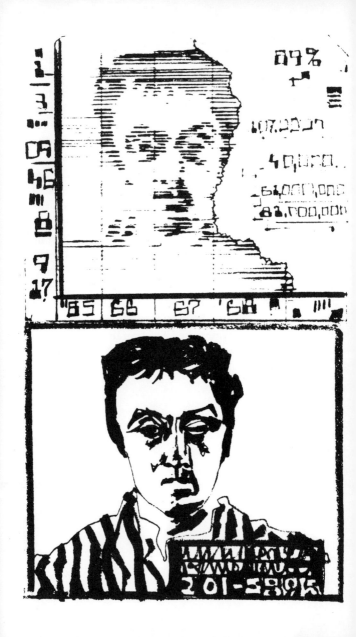

1

The Crime Problem: Myths and Realities

The growth of crime in America has caused confusion and created public fear. Citizen concern for secure streets and personal safety has resulted in the denunciation of respected officials, police frustrations, judicial stoicism, devious legal procedures, and public disrespect for the law enforcement process. Some of the tension is the result of urban growth and disorganization, but much of it comes from doubt and suspicion. Factual information, however, exposes some of the popular myths and shows that the modern crime problem to some extent seems less a social threat and more a failure of modern institutions to respond to social change. Crime and riot problems, as the President's Crime Commission and the Kerner Commission on Civil Disorders found, are inherent in the operating social system. They cannot be divorced from educational inadequacy, employment policy, race prejudice, political corruption, family hatred, police graft, court inefficiency, and general poverty. However, the true dimensions of these problems can be revealed only as we consider a number of popular myths and discuss the reality in each case.

The Myth of Modern Statistics

One myth can be stated in these words: "MODERN STATISTICS OFFER AN ACCURATE INSIGHT INTO THE CRIME PROBLEM."

This is the reality: *"The Uniform Crime Reports*

of the Federal Bureau of Investigation offer the best available source of American crime data.

Presented in tabular form, the reports categorize and itemize the criminal violations known to the police and the arrests carried out as part of the enforcement function. Since the data represent composite reports of local officers, prosecuting attorneys, court officials, and the general public, their validity depends on the accuracy of police-reporting procedures. Because the police are more likely to learn of a murder than of a successful theft, homicide information possesses greater accuracy and validity than information on shoplifting or other property crimes. Statistics on curfew and loitering violations, infrequently recorded, are even less reliable.

The popular image of modern crime is largely derived from newspaper headlines and special articles written from the data provided in the FBI's quarterly report of seven serious *Index Offenses* of murder and nonnegligent manslaughter (willful homicide), forcible rape, robbery, aggravated assault, burglary (breaking and entering), larceny of $50 or over, and auto theft. Because they assume that an extreme criminal offense will lead the victim to report an attack or major theft to the police, many people also assume, rightly or wrongly, that the *Uniform Crime Reports* are an accurate index of criminality trends. Criminologists believe that less than one third of all rapes are reported to the police and thereby to the crime index, since the victim also bears a social stigma if the crime is reported. The exact theft volume may also escape description. Several years ago Thorsten Sellin and Marvin Wolfgang found that more cases of theft were known to employees of three Philadelphia department stores than were known to the city police for the whole community.

10

While arrest statistics offer greater accuracy than the statistics on crimes known to the police, they primarily measure the volume of police activity during a specific year. The wide discrepancy between the numbers of crimes known to the police and the actual arrests of offenders confuses the problem. Although Chicago police, for example, received more than 107,000 reports of serious crimes during 1966, they completed fewer than 56,000 arrests. While enlargement of the police force would add to the arrest total, it is unreasonable to expect that all *known* crimes could ever be cleared by arrest. A detailed study of the Chicago's Town Hall Police District, for example, revealed that with nearly one seventh of all crimes reported to police during a one-week period occurrence could not be verified.

Although the *Uniform Crime Reports* represent the best available crime data, they do not give the complete picture of the total crime problem. Whole areas of organized crime and crimes committed by persons of higher status (white-collar crimes) are neglected by the *Uniform Crime Reports.* Dominated by concern for traditional crime, the *Reports* have tended to focus on those acts most often committed by lower-class members. They ignore the more sophisticated and costly crimes of the middle- and upper-class violators who may manipulate corporate stocks or practice false advertising. These forms of property violations, often handled by administrative commissions rather than criminal courts, may do as much or more social harm than many traditional property crimes of larceny, burglary, and auto theft.

Recent studies reveal that more than 90 percent of a sampled population have engaged in one or more crimes which could have culminated in successful prosecution and incarceration if discovered. Most of these persons, however, avoided detection, overcame their temporary deviancy, and became normal and respected citizens. A 1965 survey of 10,000 households by the National Opinion Research Center revealed that forcible rapes, robberies, aggravated assaults, burglaries, and larcenies of $50 or over were more commonly known to the respondent than to the police. Personal injury crime was almost twice the *UCR* rate, while property crime was more than twice the *UCR* rate for individuals. Police aid was sought least often in cases involving consumer fraud (10 percent), while auto thefts stimulated the highest (89 percent) report to police rate.

Crime, like an iceberg, hides its greatest volume below the surface. Part of the apparent crime increase is a result of greater public sensitivity to crime detection and of better reporting, standardized enforcement statistical procedures, better police enforcement patterns, and the creation of new criminal laws which lead to increased numbers of convicted offenders. Belief that particular crimes, however, are beyond police control and that contact with the police will only cause public embarrassment and personal inconvenience continues to restrain victims from reporting violations to the police.

Contrary to the myth, modern statistics do not give a completely accurate report of the crime problem.

Crime Increase Indicates a Moral Breakdown
The myth reads, "THE CRIME INCREASE INDICATES A GENERAL MORAL BREAKDOWN IN AMERICA."

The reality: *Although the public sees in the rising crime rate disintegrating moral standards, the increase is also related to the growth of the urban complex.*

In a general moral breakdown, the increase in crime would be uniformly evident in all rural or urban districts, areas, and regions. The United States, however, does not reflect such a crime pattern. Rural crime rates have remained lower than urban rates. The highest crime rates generally exist in areas of greatest social disorganization. On the other hand, cohesive communities have been most successful in meeting the crime challenge.

The largest crime increase is in the major urban Standard Metropolitan Statistical Areas which include a core population of 50,000 persons plus satellite communities. While in 1965 approximately 2 million serious index offenses known to the police were recorded in cities, 500,000 and 170,000 violations were reported by suburban and rural areas. Although the 1967 rural crime rate reached 709.2 and the suburban rates neared 1,475 violations per 100,000 residents, the 1967 urban rate exceeded 2,397 offenses known to the police. The 1967 rural crime rate, however, was less than one third the rate reported for the urban areas. While rural communities maintained a lower overall crime rate, rural murder or nonnegligent manslaughter and forcible rape rates were proportionately higher than those found among the smaller cities. Surprisingly, the rural murder rate (5.9) nearly approximated the SMSA rate of 6.6 per 100,000 population. Rural forcible rape rates, however, fell far short of the urban rate, although they remained at a higher level than evidenced by smaller cities. Robberies in 1967 were fourteen times more common in SMSA communities than in rural territories. Burglary and larceny rates were higher in the larger SMSA cities than in either the rural or smaller city categories. The wide variation in rural (61.5) and

SMSA (439.8) auto theft rates indicates that increased crime is a product of the larger urban community, which continues to grow as urban problems remain unsolved.

Low income, white overdependency, ethnic hopelessness, unstable family life, unemployment, overproportion of single males, substandard and overcrowded housing, high rates of infant mortality and disease, mixed land use, high population density, increased social vulnerability, and low ownership rates stimulate criminal activity.

Geographic and regional factors, however, also influence the nature of crime and criminal activity. Although the highly urbanized Northeastern states possessed the lowest 1967 murder rate (3.6 per 100,000), the more rural Southern states maintained a rate nearly two and one half times greater. Robbery, substantially lower in the Southern states, was nearly 25 percent higher in the Western states during 1967 (108.9 robberies per 100,000 inhabitants). Although evidencing a lower murder rate, the Northeastern states exhibited an abnormally high aggravated assault rate, indicating the probability that well-developed medical practices and facilities prevented many deaths which formerly resulted from similar aggravated assaults. While crimes against the body of the person occurred most frequently in the Southern states during 1967, arrests for crimes against property reached their highest volume in the Western areas.

Much of the crime increase has resulted from the social disorganization accompanying exploding urban growth and is not necessarily an indication of a general moral breakdown.

How Crime Is Defined

The myth says: "CRIME IS DEFINED BY PUBLIC STANDARDS OF BEHAVIOR."

The reality states: *Crimes are violations of specific laws which result in the punishment of the violator who fails to complete the act which the law requires or engages in an activity which the law prohibits.*

Although moral and ethical ideals may motivate the formation of criminal legislation, actual laws defining the criminal act do not necessarily reflect moral principles. While the Ten Commandments, for example, prohibit adultery, American criminal law and enforcement largely ignore the issue. On the other hand, young girls below a specified age (for example, 18) are protected by statutory rape legislation against a particular form of fornication (sexual intercourse between unmarried persons).

Since criminal law is highly pragmatic, emerging from human experience, it represents a lower behavioral standard than that of religious or moral idealism. Because it is directed to specific behavioral ends, criminal law may not coincide with the imperatives of the Christian life. Because a complex society involves a multiplicity of value and belief systems, criminal law represents a value compromise which all groups are expected to abide by. Criminal laws are specific. They preclude the application of broad ethical principles based on a standard of behavior which wide sections of the society might reasonably be unable to fulfill. Although criminal law serves to sustain the social structure, it reflects the emotional, value, and rational attitudes of a particular population—developing in an uneven manner. While it may be a pragmatic solution to the perceived problems of a particular period, the specific law becomes legitimized through political legislation and public acceptance.

Not public or religious concepts of morality but laws define crime.

Criminal Law as Protection

The myth says, "CRIMINAL LAW IS DESIGNED TO PROTECT THE IMMEDIATE PERSON AND HIS PROPERTY."

The reality: *Although criminal law attempts to protect the person and his property, its task is even greater.*

Any system of criminal legislation presupposes a wide variety of goals, including such diverse ends as the protection of the person against violence, cruelty, or forms of unintended harm; the protection of the easily susceptible, especially the young or feebleminded, against personal or property exploitation; the prevention of unnatural acts in the form of incest, homosexuality, bestiality; and the prevention of shocking acts in such forms as obscenity, blasphemy, nakedness, or heterosexual public copulation. Attempts to discourage behavior that might provoke disorder, incite riots, or result in personal insults are also mirrored in the criminal code. The protection of property by laws designed to prevent arson, larceny, or forgery, and the protection from inconvenience by prohibitions against falsification of records or road obstruction, however, are joined by laws designed to raise revenue through the licensing of automobiles, dogs, or bicycles. The desire to guarantee the defense of the nation and the enforcement of justice also stimulates the formation of particular criminal laws. Since criminal law evolves in response to particular social conditions, it betrays an inconsistent philosophy and needs periodic recodification and reintegration.

Criminal law serves to protect the person and his property; it also gives structure and stability to society.

Does Crime Pay?

The myth is often stated: "CRIME DOES NOT PAY."

The reality: *More than 75 percent of all known property crimes never result in an arrest.*

In essence crime is profitable as long as it does not result in physical harm for the victim. While nearly 90 percent of all crimes against the person, whether in the form of willful homicide, forcible rape, or aggravated assault, are cleared by the arrest of the offender, their clearance is largely possible because the victim is able to identify his assailant.

TABLE 1.1

NUMBER AND RATE OF ARRESTS
FOR THE 10 MOST FREQUENT OFFENSES, 1965

4,062 agencies reporting; total population 134,095,000

Rank	Offense	Number	Rate (per 100,000 population)	Percent of total arrests
1	Drunkenness	1,535,040	1,144.7	31.0
2	Disorderly conduct	570,122	425.2	11.5
3	Larceny (over and under $50)	383,726	286.2	7.7
4	Driving under the influence	241,511	180.1	4.9
5	Simple assault	207,615	154.8	4.2
6	Burglary	197,627	147.4	4.0
7	Liquor laws	179,219	133.7	3.6
8	Vagrancy	120,416	89.8	2.4
9	Gambling	114,294	85.2	2.3
10	Motor vehicle theft	101,763	75.9	2.1
	Total, 10 most frequent offenses	3,651,333	2,723.9	73.7
	Arrests for all offenses [1]	4,955,047	3,695.2	100.0

[1] Does not include arrests for traffic offenses.
Source: *Uniform Crime Reports—1965*, pp. 108–109.

Crimes of larceny and burglary are harder to detect. A large portion of current property crime is encouraged by modern business practices. Open merchandise displays encourage both compulsive buying and compulsive shoplifting. Since fewer than 15 of every 100 criminal violations ever result in the successful prosecution of the alleged offended, the risk of apprehension and incarceration is minimized.

Contrary to the myth, crime does pay for all undetected offenders.

Are Neighborhoods Unsafe?

The myth says: "THERE HAS BEEN SUCH AN INCREASE IN MURDER AND RAPE THAT EVERY NEIGHBORHOOD IS UNSAFE."

The reality: *While murder and rape are feared by many people and looked upon as major evidences of crime increase, they are really a small percentage of the total crime volume.*

Obsessive concern for these forms of crime may actually hinder the development of more realistic full-scale enforcement since the emotion provoked by both crimes clouds the larger issue of successful and more costly forms of organized, white-collar, and property crimes. Although murder and rape involve major threat and harm for the individual, heavier costs and greater volume of crime activity are borne by those facing property violations. Fewer than 12,000 willful homicides occurred among an approximate 1967 population of 205,000,000 Americans. At the same time, suicides approximated 20,000, while auto deaths involved nearly 50,000 persons. Although approximately 128 serious assaults for every 100,000 inhabitants occurred during 1967, more than 12,000 home accidents per 100,000 residents were recorded during the same period. While an estimated 27,000 forcible rapes were reported to the police in 1967, most criminologists believe that another 34 to 40 thousand escaped detection since a report would lead to added stigma. The greatest numbers of murders occur between persons who formerly shared a courtship, marriage, or homosexual love relationship. Rape victims, too, often know their assailants. Preliminary studies suggest that more than 40 percent of the female rape victims shared in the conditions leading to their personal violation. Because his action is largely determined by his relationship to the victim, the murderer has the greatest potential for rehabilitation. The rapist, on the other hand, is a behavioral type deeply in need of psychiatric aid and is seldom detected before the crime has been committed. Violent crimes, however, still remain a mere fraction of the total crime picture. Their very infrequency makes them "news," while the more common theft and burglary remain unreported by the press.

The facts do not support the conclusion that every neighborhood is unsafe as a result of increases in murder and rape.

Arrest and Guilt

In the thinking of many people, "THE ARREST OF AN ALLEGED OFFENDER IMPLIES GUILT."

The reality: *American criminal law operates on the principle that a man is innocent until proved guilty.* No guilt, therefore, exists until the evidence of the crime has been presented and a judgment has been rendered. Since the law assumes that the individual violator must possess the ability to reason or to form a guilty mind (*mens rea*), the court attempts to ascertain whether the individual violator has complete command of his mental faculties. Because criminal law makes a basic distinction between an intended and an accidental act, the system of justice seeks to determine individual criminal intent. If any particular act was intended and apparent to the mind of the criminal, the court assumes that the man invoked a rational decision that led him to commit his original act. If the man was incapable of intent due to insanity, senility, or other acceptable alternative, intent is deemed impossible, and an alternative judgment is rendered. Many acts, however, fall midway between these two extremes. American criminal law, for example, assumes that any person committing a criminal act while drunk completes a rational act, since he obviously intended to drink and, by extension of his drinking, to complete an intended criminal act.

A man is not guilty until proved so in court.

Relation of Known Crimes to Arrest

The myth reads, "CRIMES KNOWN TO THE POLICE RESULT IN ARRESTS AND CONVICTIONS."

The reality: *A gradual shrinkage in the total known crime volume occurs at each stage of the enforcement, adjudication, and correctional process.*

The number of convicted offenders, as a result, represents a mere fraction of the total number of crimes committed. Murder and nonnegligent manslaughter offer the highest crime arrest (clearance) rate. While nearly 89 percent of known murders and nonnegligent manslaughters were cleared by the arrest of some offender, less than 61 percent of reported forcible rapes resulted in the arrest of an alleged offender in 1967. Aggravated assault and other serious visible crimes against the person, however, possessed a slightly higher clearance rate, since a large proportion of victims and offenders were known to each other. Fewer than 30 percent of all known robberies, on the other hand, were cleared by the arrest of an alleged offender in 1967, suggesting the major success robbers possess. While each of the seven index categories evidenced a similar percentage of 1967 arrests which resulted in an eventual charge (varying from more than 65 to 78 percent), the number of adult acquittals and dismissals ranged from nearly 13 percent in cases of larceny to an approximate 35 percent for forcible rape.

The lack of juvenile sophistication in robbery, burglary, larceny, and auto theft plays a large factor in the disproportionate number of juvenile arrests. The greater number of juvenile or adult property offenders, however, are never arrested or convicted. The highest 1967 conviction rate occurred in the crime of drunkenness (nearly 88 percent), while the lowest rate was reported for arson (15.2 percent of those formally charged by the police). While nearly 48 percent of all persons charged for tabulated index offenses in 1967 were eventually referred to the juvenile court, approximately 31 percent of all serious index-crime offenders were judged guilty as charged. Juvenile referrals for all reported crimes, however, declined to less than 18 percent, indicating the disproportionate involvement of juveniles in serious crimes.

Contrary to the myth, only a small percentage of all offenders are arrested and eventually convicted.

Crime and Age Group
The myth says, "INCREASE IN CRIME VOLUME IS EQUAL IN ALL AGE GROUPS."

The reality: *The disproportionate number of juve-*

niles arrested for serious criminal acts reveals the major problems inherent in modern education, family life, and career employment.

Juvenile delinquency is a forerunner to adult crime. The earlier the juvenile's arrest or contact with the juvenile court, the more likely will be his participation in serious adult criminal activity. The more serious his first offense, the greater his likelihood to continue in serious, especially property crime. The more frequently he is processed by the police, the juvenile court, and the correctional system, the greater is the likelihood that he will be arrested, charged, and imprisoned as an adult.

Persons *under 25* accounted for nearly half of all 1967 arrests. Surprisingly, juveniles under 15 were arrested for nearly 50 percent of vandalism, 47 percent of arson, 26 percent of burglaries, 25 percent of curfew and loitering violations, and lesser percents in all remaining crime categories. Individuals *25 years and over*, however, accounted for 63 percent of all 1967 arrests for murder and nonnegligent manslaughter, nearly 37 percent of rape, approximately 27 percent of robbery, slightly more than 56 percent of aggravated assault, less than 18 percent of burglary, approximately 23 percent of larceny, and 12 percent of auto theft. The greatest 1960–66 arrest increases occurred among youth 18 years of age, reflecting the problems of juvenile and young adult adjustment to modern society.

Contrary to the myth, crime reflects the problems of youth and the community.

Female Crime

The myth says, "FEMALE CRIME IS INSIGNIFICANT."

The reality: *Females are arrested one seventh as often as the male population for all seven index offenses and larceny under $50.*

The wide variation in male and female arrest rates, however, is declining as females commit crimes at a faster rate. Between 1960 and 1965 the male arrest rate increased by 18 percent while the female rate increased by a substantial 62 percent. The major increase during this period, however, was due to the 81 percent rise in female larceny arrests. The next highest female arrest category of aggravated assault increased by only 4 percent. Although females accounted for less than 13 percent of all persons arrested during 1966, the low female crime and arrest rates may be due to traditional definitions of female roles and the greater protection afforded females by American society.

Female crime has risen sharply in recent years.

Negroes and Crime
The myth says, "NEGROES COMMIT MORE CRIME THAN WHITES."

The reality: *White Americans dominate the yearly arrest figures, although Negro Americans evidence a significantly higher arrest rate in every crime category with the exception of offenses against public order and against morals.* The 1965 Negro rate for all index offenses plus larceny under $50 was four times the rate of the white population (1,696 to 419 violations per 100,000 persons). The disproportionate Negro arrest rate, possibly partly due to police prejudice and discrimination in some areas, was not completely sustained by court conviction. While the white arrest rate for murder reached only 2.5 per 100,000 persons in 1965, the Negro arrest rate was nearly ten times higher (24.1). Although burglary arrests were less extreme, Negroes evidenced a burglary rate more than three times greater than the 1965 white rate. Although Negroes numbered less than 11 percent of the American population, Negro youth under 18 were arrested nearly three times as often as whites (1,689 to 591 arrests per 100,000 persons). Negroes over 18, however, revealed an even higher proportion, reaching a rate approximately five times the white rate. Although the Negro arrest rate for murder, rape, and aggravated assault, already high, increased by only 5 percent between 1960−65, the white rate increased by 27 percent. While Negro robberies, on the other hand, increased by 24 percent, the white rate grew only 3 percent during the same period.

Crime is the monopoly of no single racial group.

Interracial Attacks

The myth suggests, "WHITES ARE MOST LIKELY TO BE SUBJECTED TO NEGRO ATTACK."

The reality: *A 1965 Chicago police department study of 13,713 cases of nonhomicide assaultive crimes found that the Negro male and female were the most likely victims of crime against the person.* Although the Chicago Negro male was the victim nearly six times as often as the white male, the Negro female became the victim almost eight times as often as the white female. Negroes were most likely to assault Negroes, and whites to assault whites. A 1966 survey by the District of Columbia Crime Commission revealed similar findings. Less than 7 percent (12) of the 172 D. C. murders and 20 percent of recorded Washington rapes were interracial in character. Two thirds of all auto theft victims were Negro. Robbery was the only crime of violence in which the majority of the victims, 56 percent, were white. Recent increase in racial tension may in the future give some reality to the myth.

In most instances the victim of a crime against the person is of the same race.

Victims and Social Classes

The myth states, "ALL SOCIAL CLASSES ARE THE VICTIMS OF CRIME."

The reality: *While technically true, crime and victimization most frequently occur among the lower classes.* Although aggravated assault, larceny, and auto theft victims are more representative of the general white population, forcible rapes, robbery, and burglary victims are especially concentrated among the lowest income groups. Larceny victims are most likely to come from the highest income categories. Nonwhites, however, are disproportionate victims in all crime categories, with the exception of larcenies of $50 and over. Among women, the 20−29 age group are the most frequently victimized, especially in crimes involving forcible rape or robbery. Although property-crime victims are found among males of all ages, male aggravated assault and robbery victims are most often between 20 and 29 years of age.

Although crime is frequent also among middle- and upper-class members, lower-class citizens are most likely to be arrested for violations of current laws.

Crime and Seasonal Changes

The myth holds, "SEASONAL CHANGES HAVE LITTLE CONNECTION WITH CRIME PATTERNS."

The reality: *Weather and other sociocultural factors associated with seasonal changes influence crime patterns.*

While murder occurs most frequently during July and December, being stimulated by such diverse factors as summer heat, Christmas arguments, and uncontrolled drinking patterns, forcible rape and aggravated assault reach their peak during the summer months when sexual stimulation and group contact are most common. Negligent manslaughter increases sharply in November and December, affected by snow and icy roads. Although robbery increases during the early fall, as days become shorter and fewer persons venture into the darkness, a sharp decline in robbery during the months of January to March is partially due to weather conditions which encourage indoor activity. Burglaries and larcenies follow similar patterns, becoming more pronounced in August and December. Property crimes tend to increase during the summer months when families are vacationing, fewer employees are on duty, stores are crowded, and mobility is enhanced.

Although season changes influence the crime rate, other factors are more important and influential in crime causation.

Organized Crime

The myth states, "ORGANIZED CRIME IS INSIGNIFICANT."

The reality: *Since organized crime offers services to reputable citizens under monopoly conditions, it possesses the power to corrupt law enforcement or political officials and to undermine the general tone of a particular community.* Operating in marginal areas of gambling, narcotics, prostitution, labor racketeering, and usury, organized crime attempts to maximize profits while minimizing risks as it serves a significant minority of the so-called legitimate population. While the public believes that traditional crime offers the major threat to society, the financial volume of organized crime is twice that of traditional crime forms. The public over-sensitivity to traditional crimes has caused the populace to ignore the costs and corruption of organized criminality. Organized crime cannot exist without the collusion of politicians, racketeers, lawyers, enforcement officials, accountants, and *the general public.* Organized as a form of big business, syndicate crime offers marginal services prohibited by law to persons, often members of the lower class, who are willing to purchase its basic goods and services.

The costs of organized crime are high, although the public is generally unaware of the implications of this crime form.

Solution by Law and Punishment

The myth holds, "ALL THAT IS NEEDED TO SOLVE THE CRIME PROBLEM ARE STRICTER LAWS AND HARSHER PUNISHMENTS."

The reality: *The continuing crime increase witnesses that this historic approach, in effect since earliest times, has had minimal success.* Criminologists now recognize that the control of crime is best achieved by swift and certain punishment rather than by harsh laws or lengthy incarceration. The philosophy of harsher laws and stricter punishments obscures the functional nature of modern crime and allows the public to avoid its responsibility for law enforcement and court reform, equipment modernization, salary increases for enforcement personnel, and effective treatment and correctional programs. Lower-class respect for law and order is hardly encouraged by the wide prevalence of organized and white-collar crime, court overcrowding, poor legal representation, or arbitrary or judicial actions which violate elementary concepts of justice. Current incarceration procedures place the convicted criminal in touch with a greater density of known criminals than could ever be achieved in his own community. Until new philosophical and social concepts replace the traditional approach to criminal deviance, crime will continue to increase as the public piously ignores the problem of crime causation.

The treatment goal has never been realized. The attempt to control human behavior by legal means has not been uniformly successful.

Criminal Justice and Rehabilitation

The myth says, "THE SYSTEM OF CRIMINAL JUSTICE IS ORIENTED TO THE REHABILITATION OF THE OFFENDER."

The reality: *Between 85 and 90 percent of all enforcement costs involve wages and salaries, leaving a very small proportion for police-force modernization, evaluative research, or rehabilitation attempts.* Even though crime prevention and control costs an estimated $4 billion a year, only a small proportion of money expended for criminal justice is ever allotted to rehabilitation programs designed to effect basic changes in criminal personalities. Law enforcement correctional institutions continue to operate at substandard levels of need and efficiency at a time of peak criminal incarceration. The assumption that the best treatment occurs in large-scale isolation centers (prisons), theoretically questionable in itself, results in higher enforcement and correctional expense. If people knew that the adult offender can best be rehabilitated with the least cost (less than 50 cents per day) in his own community, an immediate reexamination of the process of justice would take place. Treatment by a local psychiatrist working in cooperation with a community probation officer carrying a small case load, for example, can be more effective than the current approach which places marginal offenders in a penal institution of 1,600 inmates, served by one or two psychologists; here costs are more than ten times as high.

The public must assume a major part of the responsibility for the crime increase, since it has continually refused to fund adequate staff, equipment, and research and has tied the hands of enforcement bodies by legislation designed to maintain traditional myths and to restrict creative correctional programs. The need to rethink the community approach to juvenile delinquency is quite evident. The President's Commission on Law Enforcement and Administration of Justice found, for example, that by the 1970s more than 40 percent of the male population will have experienced one or more contacts with the juvenile courts. The mere fact that a substantial portion of the population has come to the attention of the juvenile court indicates the dimensions of the juvenile problem and the unwillingness of the community to deal with the basic needs of the significant juvenile population. The promise of the juvenile court has never materialized.

The popular fallacies concerning the crime problem merely compound the issues involved. Since the costs of error in handling the criminal or crime are so great, the public has been unwilling to experiment with new techniques of crime control or with recent discoveries concerning methods of treatment. The search for solutions, however, can not be detached from the attempt to understand the causes of crime.

While crime throughout human history has been explained in terms of demons, mental instability, poverty, group conflict, free will, or other sociopsychological causes, the quest for understanding continues. No solution, however, will ever be found until myth has been replaced by reality, and fear with hope.

2
The Causes of Crime

Any attempt to prevent or control crime ultimately involves an evaluation of crime causes. Some primitive societies attributed the criminal act to the presence of demons within the person. Contemporary theorists have been unable to define the explicit relationship between a person, his social environment, and the criminal act. Major attempts to ascertain crime causes have occurred in the last 200 years, beginning with the development of the classical school of criminological theory.

Classical Theory

Cesare Bonesana, Marchese de Beccaria, opened the scientific investigation of crime causation in the latter half of the 18th century. Rejecting the belief that crime was caused by demons or inherent evil spirits, Beccaria theorized that hedonistic, pleasure-seeking impulses led to criminal acts. Arguing that man is endowed with the capacity to express his free will through his rational choices, Beccaria theorized that a criminal seeks to avoid pain in order to attain that which is self-satisfying. Crime, he held, is best controlled by rendering punishment in place of pleasure. If each quantum of crime were punished by an adequate quantum of punishment, criminal activity would be deterred. Since the severity of each crime differs, murder being more serious than a theft of property, punishment should be devised to fit the crime in order to balance the scales of justice.

Although Beccaria's *classical theory* of necessity

focused on the crime as a *legal* act, his followers tended to ignore the intent and personal behavior of the criminal violator. Believing the question of the person's intent to commit the crime to be irrelevant, Beccaria attached significance only to the actual violation which led to criminal prosecution and punishment. While his idea was revolutionary in its day, Beccaria's theory ignored the basic sociocultural dimensions of the crime and focused on a strict legal interpretation. Motivated by the desire to overcome the injustices of the Italian courts which came with the uncontrolled use of judicial power, Beccaria and his followers emphasized an exact punishment for a specific crime. Although the Beccarian interpretation has long been dismissed by social thinkers and criminologist-penologists, contemporary public attitudes sometimes still reflect this viewpoint.

The Positivist School

Physician-psychiatrist Cesare Lombroso opposed Beccaria's interpretation and established a *positivist school of criminology* in the last quarter of the 1800s. Contradicting the legalistic view of Beccaria, Lombroso and the positivists held that the causes of criminal behavior were hidden in psychological and social factors. Heavily influenced by the doctrine of evolution in vogue in 1876, the positivists believed that they could identify potential offenders through facial, cephalic, or body irregularities. A criminal, Lombroso originally wrote, was a primitive type of man who frequently possessed physical and psychological characteristics which encouraged his criminal tendency. Many were *born criminals*, Lombroso at first thought, an idea which Beccaria supported by his discovery that more than one half of the criminals of his day were insane or criminaloid, the latter consisting of individuals predisposed to crime by hereditary physical and psychological characteristics which would become public under peculiar environmental conditions.

The Polar Positions of the Two Schools

The differences in classical and positivistic viewpoints have continued to the present day in modified form. Although representing two polar positions, the Beccarian and Lombrosian schools in a way set the limits of the continuing attempt to define the causes of crime. The classical school defined crime in legal terms, but the positivists rejected a legal definition of criminality, assuming that crime is a product of physical, psychological, and social conditions. Although the classicists focused on crime as a legal entity, the positivists held that the criminal act represents a psychological unit. While the classical school emphasized individual free will and rational choice in the commission of the criminal act, the positivists emphasized a form of social determinism which recognized that each person makes choices in relationship to social-environmental alternatives that differ according to sex, social class, racial or ethnic identifications, or other variable factors. Although the classical school believed punishment possessed a deterrent effect as it replaced pleasure with pain, the positivists argued that punishment is obsolete and should be replaced by scientific treatment which can both protect society and treat the criminal.

Lombroso's initial assumption that certain physical types (born criminals) more readily engage in criminal activity led to the formulation of additional theories which held that criminal tendencies were related to physical peculiarities or abnormalities. Believing that variations in biological structures cause differential behavior, later *physical type* theorists ignored the psychological and social characteristics of the person in favor of physical abnormalities.

Johan Lavater, proponent of *physiognomy*, claimed that crime was most likely to be expressed by beardless men, bearded women, or persons affected by a "shifty" eye, a "weak" chin, or an "arrogant" nose. *Phrenologist* Franz Joseph Gall, a European anatomist, related crime to head conformation and mental faculties. Although the phrenologists sought to explain their crime theory through the Aristotelian idea that the brain serves as the "organ of the mind," their inability to validate their hypotheses led to the later rejection of their work.

Defective Intelligence

The attempts to explain crime through differences in physical body types or head size were quickly rejected when evidence did not support these assumptions, but the belief that crime was caused by low intelligence persisted. The attempt to prove the existence of this relationship led to the development of Binet's I. Q. studies, which tried to differentiate various levels of innate intelligence, separating the imbecile from the genius. Although the *defective intelligence* explanation assumed that crime results when potential offenders are not intelligent enough to understand the hazardous nature of crime or to perceive the satisfying reward of a normal law-abiding life, its presuppositions could not be scientifically proved by tests conducted among incarcerated criminals. Al Murchison found that prisoners in five states performed consistently better on the administered intelligence test than many groups of World

War I draftees. Other researchers found that feeble-mindedness was a minimal crime influence since the proportion of feebleminded persons in penal institutions was not significantly larger than that of the general population. Later tests revealed that the criminal population, while evidencing less formal education, reflected similar intelligence distributions as found among the "normal" population.

Mental and Emotional Disorders

Although later theorists attempted to explain criminality in terms of *defective inheritance, endocrine imbalance, or multiple factors influencing the transmission of heredity,* the parallel emergence of psychology and psychiatry brought new theories relating crime to *mental* and *emotional disorders.* Insanity was redefined as an illness rather than a form of rational behavior subject to control through punishment. Because insanity rendered the person incapable of choosing between right and wrong, the *psychiatric theorists* rejected the assumption that a man unable to form a criminal intent could be guilty of an illegal act which assumed a rational will. Since English common law had earlier taken for granted that any child under the age of seven could not commit a felony because he was incapable of forming an intent, the concept was merely extended to include persons judged insane — a legal attempt to define a psychological condition.

As Sigmund Freud attempted to explain the context of all human behavior, his interpretations led to new theories of crime causation. Although certain portions of the personality which create basic mental conflicts within the person are repressed into the individual's unconscious, the ideas, impulses or complexes, the

37

Freudian School maintained, continue to exist in the unconscious and may periodically find expression in dreams or other forms of social, antisocial, or symbolic behavior. Criminal activity, therefore, may be a substitute response to repressed complexes, conflicts of the unconscious mind, or feelings of guilt and anxiety which seek punishment in order to restore the proper balance between definitions of good and evil; Freud in essence assumed that the violator commits criminal acts in order to be caught and punished. Other psychiatric interpretations offered a similar theoretical view, holding that criminal behavior is merely an extension of basic personality patterns.

Economic Causes

The inability of psychological or psychiatric theorists to explain all forms of criminal behavior, however, led to a wide variety of other attempts to explain the causes of crime. Because crime by definition is a violation of laws which may vary from society to society, these explanations attempted to place the criminal act within its social context.

The *Marxian theory of economic determinism*, for example, assumed that crime is related to economic ideology and practice. Since the production, distribution, consumption, and exchange of goods and services dominate the major activities of most human beings, criminal activity is merely a deviant extension of this influence. Because theft involves the stealing of property, its basic goal is economic. Therefore criminal activity, Marxist theorists argued, can only be reduced when state ownership of all important property and state economic planning replace all concepts of individual or corporate private property ownership. Crime, they believed, is a product of economic maladjustment which will only diminish when all social classes share in equal economic opportunities.

The Marxian idea, however, finds no support in data which reveals that poverty does not automatically lead to crime and that recorded criminal activity reaches its highest volume in the more technological and affluent societies.

Group Conflict

In contrast to Marxist determinism, group-conflict crime explanations say that personality is formed through a process of social interaction. Man, conflict theorists suppose, is a product of his group associations. Since each group is forced to maintain, defend, or enhance its own position within the mass society, conflict naturally occurs. Because human groups are formed by persons who share common interests or needs and who come together for further collective action, attempts to maintain group positions may result periodically in conflict between nations, races, religious-economic systems, unions, or other groups and organizations. Since each group seeks to maximize its power, it ultimately tries to gain group advantages and minimize potential opposition through the legislative process. Some types of crime, therefore, are attempts by a significant group or groups to obtain some of the power of the prevailing group.

Organized crime has its roots in the attempt of criminal syndicates to maximize profits through the creation of business monopolies. Minimizing risks, organized crime operates in conflict with legitimate business and provides illegal goods or services to customers at a fee. Although traditionally structured to provide illicit services, organized crime has more recently moved to infiltrate legitimate business and to gain commodity distribution control, creating profits through a monopoly of a particular item (for example, olive oil). Offering marginal or even necessary services, the syndicates can only exist in collusion with corrupt public officials, local lawyers, public accountants, law enforcement officers, and public prosecutors and are in conflict with the public.

Multiple Factors as Crime Causes

Modern theorists assume that crime involves multiple factors and can no longer be explained in terms of one particular physical, psychological, or social factor.

Abrahamsen's Psychiatric Variation Formula

David Abrahamsen believes that crime causes are relative. Criminal behavior (C) emerges in relationship to the individual's tendency to commit a particular act (T), the situation (S) in which he finds himself, and the person's mental and emotional ability to resist temptation (R). Therefore criminal behavior can be reduced to the formula: $\frac{C=T+S}{R}$. Inherent in his *psychiatric variation formula* is the assumption that all persons have criminal impulses which *may or may not* issue in criminal acts, depending upon the criminal opportunity and their sense of self-discipline and personal stability. Although criminal tendencies may be revealed in emotional instability, overpowering drives, or even asocial attitudes and feelings, Abrahamsen holds that crime is a composite response of social conditioning and personal need.

Carr's Deviation Differential Theory

Lowell J. Carr is even more explicit. Individuals, Carr argues, either conform or fail to conform to their existing environment in relation to the quality and intensity of the negative psychological and environmental processes which affect them. Each person is confronted with conforming and deviating factors which involve both psychological and environmental dimensions. If *conforming factors* (CF) outweigh deviating factors, the *conforming differential* (CD) leads to *conforming behavior* (CB). On the other hand, if *deviating factors* (DF) outweigh the conforming factors, the *deviating differential* (DD) leads to *deviating behavior* (DB). The *psychological* (I) and *environmental* (E) characteristics, therefore, are influenced by the conforming or deviating factors. Reducing this theory to formula form, Carr suggests:

$$CF(I \times E) - DF(I \times E) = \begin{cases} CD \\ or \\ DD \end{cases} \begin{array}{l} \longrightarrow CB \\ \\ \longrightarrow DB \end{array}$$

Although the theory fails to explain how maladjusted personalities become delinquent, it suggests that criminal behavior is a product of many varied factors.

Bloch's Psychogenic View

Herbert Bloch theorizes that crime is a reflection of the personality structure which is primarily determined by class, subcultural, or ethnic conditions which define culturally oriented needs or functions that are internalized within the individual's personality structure. As the individual attempts to satisfy his culturally defined needs, he may express behavior which reveals his inability to conform to normative role demands. These broad personality structures, understood as *social tropisms*, determine the individual's movement *toward* and *away from* other individuals. Although classified as egoistic, aggressive, withdrawal, or isolation personality states, these personality structures serve as *tendencies to action*. These tendencies really determine human behavior, because they express the view the individual has of himself, and he usually acts in accordance with that view (or self-concept). The cultural conditions confronting his self-concept or personality structure will either reinforce or reject his view of himself.

Criminality occurs, according to Bloch's assumption, when the individual is continually exposed to primary (or intimate) relationships involving criminal or illegal behavior — or — when the individual is placed into situations which do not agree with his image of himself and arouse feelings of tension and conflict. Then criminal patterns may be assumed and the individual engages in criminal activity. He wishes to resolve the conflict and tension between his self-concept and the actual social situation. Although Bloch's theory has not been adequately tested, it assumes that criminal behavior is part of the functioning personality and social structure, and therefore is not a radical departure from general human behavior.

Sutherland's Differential Association and Learning Theory

Criminologist Edwin Sutherland views crime as a product of human learning and group relations. Recognizing the wide diversity of criminal expressions, Sutherland divides his theory into seven integral phases.

1. Criminal behavior is learned, whether in the form of habitual, professional, organized, or white-collar criminality.

2. Social interaction and communication are central to the learning process.

3. Criminal behavior is acquired through participation in intimate personal groups, as opposed to simple contact with mass media and formal agencies or institutions.

4. The learning process involves the learning of techniques for committing crime and the formation of new attitudes, motives, drives, and forms of rationalization, evidenced in a systematic reinforcement toward criminality.

5. The specific direction of motives and drives is learned from legal definitions of favorable or unfavorable acts.

6. Delinquency occurs because definitions *favorable* to violations of the law exceed definitions *unfavorable* to violations of the law. These definitions, however, are usually reinforced by group commitments or associational relationships which the individual has established.

7. Since the degree of individual participation in the group may vary, factors of intensity, priority, duration, and frequency determine the actual tendencies toward criminal behavior.

8. All the mechanisms of learning are involved in learning criminal or anticriminal behavior.

9. Criminal and noncriminal behavior are expressions of the same needs and/or values and, therefore, cannot be explained in terms of variable needs and/or values.

Contrary to public opinion, crime, Sutherland concluded, is learned in a systematic manner by persons associating with deviant groups. Although some crimes (for example, murder and rape) may involve a mental or emotional disturbance which operates independently of group relationships, most crimes tend to be products of group commitment or subcultural conditions.

The Problem of Crimes Which Are Not Crimes

Not all acts which are harmful to society are always defined as crimes. While theft of a radio from a store is likely to be punished by court action, a theft of the consumer's money through misrepresentation of goods and commodities may be ignored by law. The problem of business violations, crimes which are often noncrimes, led Edwin Sutherland to develop the concept of *white-collar crime* to describe the forms of crime committed in the process of legitimate business activity. Because modern business practices, Sutherland believed, stimulate criminal activity which is often undetected and unreported, traditional crime categories do not adequately describe the vast number of deviant acts which are neither traditional crimes nor products of organized criminality. Because law reflects the traditional control of the propertied classes, Sutherland theorized that crime statistics traditionally itemize those crimes committed by members of the lower economic and underprivileged classes. Harmful business practices, largely restricted to persons possessing or administering property interests, are in turn controlled by noncriminal administrative boards which generally exempt more costly business crime from criminal prosecution.

These forms of white-collar criminality include such acts as misrepresentation of corporate financial statements, inflation of the stock exchange, bribery of public officials to secure desired contracts or immunities, bribery through commercial transactions, misrepresentation in salesmanship and advertising, embezzlement, misuse of funds, illegal bankruptcy, and income tax evasion. Sutherland argued that these violations of criminal law were committed by persons of the upper socioeconomic classes in the course of their occupational activity. Since these special violators are often respected community leaders, the probability of their arrest and successful prosecution is automatically minimized except in cases involving serious assaults. Although Sutherland's concept has been openly challenged by many lawyers and criminologists, his theory of white-collar crime reveals a larger context of the crime problem.

Conclusion

Modern theory and contemporary data suggest that crime is part of the social fabric. We can no longer affirm that the causes of crime are mental defects, lack of intelligence, physical deformities, poverty, or simple ignorance. Crime is evident in all classes and among all ethnic groups. The criminal is not only a lower class, uneducated, unskilled, and unemployed person. He is also the white-collar criminal in business and the underworld criminal in organized crime.

Social sciences help us understand the social, personal, and environmental influences as causes of crime, but as Christians we cannot agree that these constitute the complete cause. The Biblical view of man is an important part of the Christian understanding of crime and the criminal.

The Scriptures describe man as a fallen creature, alienated from God by his own disobedience. His sinful and fallen condition makes him self-centered and out of harmony with other people in society. "Out of the heart," as Jesus says, "proceed evil thoughts, murders, adulteries, thefts, false witness, blasphemies." The underlying cause of crime, from a Christian viewpoint, is the sinful nature of man who is separated from God.

This attitude is changed when man comes into a living relationship to God through Jesus Christ. The Spirit of God leads man to faith in Christ. In Christ man becomes a new being, ready and willing to serve God and neighbor. By the Gospel of Christ man is reconciled to God and reconciled to live in service to people.

3

Rights of the Individual and Rights of the Group

Does society have the right to supersede the rights of the individual? Who has the authority to make this decision? Under what circumstances?

These questions are critical because criminal law has been used to suppress political minorities, social programs, racial equality, and even religious expression.

The rights of the individual and of the group must exist in a delicate balance. An overemphasis on individual rights at the expense of group security can lead to anarchy and self-indulgence. Conversely, an excessive demand for group security may lead to totalitarianism and a loss of individual creativity. Neither is in the best interests of the person or the society. An overreaction to crime myths could easily lead the reactor to a totalitarian solution to the problem. An excessive focus on nebulous crime causes may lead the evaluator to take no action at all to guarantee the demands for societal security. The modern debates over civil disobedience, legalized abortion, publication of pornography, use of marijuana, legalization of wiretapping and rights to fair trial, legal counsel, and juvenile due process involve individual and group rights.

The citizen's response to these issues, however, is largely determined by his own vested interests. Civil disobedience is difficult to understand unless one is a member of a minority group; the issue of abortion, unless one has incurred an unwanted pregnancy; the problem of pornography, unless one's children have been exposed to lewd and lascivious materials; the debate about wiretapping, unless one's home and private communications have been invaded; the question of fair trial, unless one has been victimized by the press; the right to counsel, unless one has been coerced to make an untrue confession; the guarantee of due process in juvenile court, unless one has been institutionalized for a longer period than the adult offender in the name of "rehabilitation."

Truth is not limited to one side in these issues. The reality is more often found in a choice between conflicting or variable alternatives. Although a civil rights march may provoke neighborhood conflict, no conflict can exist unless community members opposing the march violate the right of the demonstrators to march, thereby breaking the peace by their own action in the name of community stability. Each of these issues is a product of human interaction within the social structure; none can be divorced from acting and reacting human beings or from the sociolegal structure of society. Laws, however, are products of legislative action; they reflect the basic concerns of those utilizing legislative power. Groups seeking to preserve their own goals have effectively used legal procedures to advance their vested interests, often at the expense of the general society. Because laws change with the redefinition of social values and needs, they represent an attempt to define minimal behavioral standards and to reduce competing group conflict through compromise. The growth of the mass society, therefore, has introduced new legislation and revised legal interpretations designed to encourage long-term social reintegration during a period of major social conflict and readjustment. The attempt to clarify the rights of the individual and the power of the group compound the tensions of the modern period.

Civil Disobedience

Modern nonviolent protest or civil-rights movements have generally been much less violent than the colonist responses to English tax laws, the protests over slavery eventuating in the Civil War, anti-Prohibition demonstrations, suffragette marches, or labor-management conflicts in previous history. Many persons outside of or on the fringe of contemporary civil-rights movements have exceeded the bounds of legitimate protest and have participated in rioting, but they have not acted in civil disobedience. Their actions were rather emotion-stimulated violation of the criminal code—often due to minority distrust of the police. Civil disobedience to test the validity of a law in a court of law is guaranteed in the Constitution; it may serve to protect both the individual and society. Rioting, on the other hand, is illegal behavior which threatens the broader society and is punishable through prosecutions in criminal courts.

The central issue in civil disobedience is not whether individual or group protest is possible but rather to determine at what point legitimate protest has passed beyond the bounds of constitutional guarantees. Although the U. S. Supreme Court consistently ruled in favor of those using the sit-in in the attempt to gain access to public accommodations, holding that the government must serve the total public rather than simply the power structure, the Court has increasingly moved to prohibit violence or arrogant displays of power.

Civil ordinances which were often enacted to restrict the assembly of minority groups protesting believed injustice were consistently reversed by the Court on the ground that the Fourteenth Amendment permits the citizen the right to challenge discriminatory legislation through peaceful demonstrations. The Court in effect recognized that laws are not static but evolve as social conditions change. Since they flow from the public will, legal codes are modified as public attitudes force adjustments.

By maintaining that the First Amendment freedoms of free speech and free assembly are inherent individual and group rights that take priority over coercive local ordinances, the Supreme Court in effect upheld the Constitution. If existing laws, the Court reasoned, are designed to limit the dissemination of ideas, the laws are unconstitutional. Local officials, however, possess the right to decide questions of time, place, duration, and manner or usage of public facilities as long as their judgment is equally and uniformly applied to all social groups in the public interest. The Court accordingly has ruled that no future demonstration, whether commendable or peaceful, will be tolerated if it violates properly drawn statutes designed to promote law and order, regulate traffic, offer community stability, maintain legitimate private property, or guarantee the proper administration of government and justice.

The crucial question involved in the issue of civil disobedience is the validity of the law which is being challenged. Since laws are finally validated by social acceptance and court clarification, their potential value depends on the willingness of the people and the courts to support the prescribed legislation. Because the U. S. Supreme Court accepts only actual rather than hypothetical cases for judgment, the legal test of an unjust law can take place only *after* an act of disobedience to the law has occurred. The American court process demands that a law be openly broken before an evaluatory judgment concerning the law can be given.

Many cases coming to the Supreme Court from the lower courts are fundamental tests of laws, convictions, or court judgments. The difference between a governor standing in the doorway to prohibit the integration of a public university and a Negro demonstrator sitting at a lunch counter in an attempt to integrate the facility is the difference between a refusal to obey a previous Supreme Court judgment directing the integration of the university and an attempt to test a local ordinance directed against a specific minority group. If law is to be respected, it must serve both the majority and the minority, the person and the group. Only then can present tensions directly related to the previous unequal application of coercive laws and ordinances be overcome.

Wiretapping and Electronic Eavesdropping

Although the arguments for legalized wiretapping and electronic eavesdropping have centered on their use in controlling organized crime, the general public has a stake in their use. The widespread use of wiretapping and electronic eavesdropping devices has forced modern society to evaluate their potential social value or threat. The police facing the frustrations of inadequate equipment, insufficient manpower, and limited public support periodically issue cries which suggest that murderers are being turned loose at rapid rates, rapists are commonly freed rather than incarcerated, society is generally protecting the criminal at the expense of the public, and legalized wiretapping and electronic eavesdropping equipment are necessary to control organized crime. The use of wiretapping and electronic eavesdropping equipment, however, involves basic constitutional questions pertaining to the invasion of personal privacy and to the admissibility of such evidence in a criminal court. Those who fear the totalitarian control of the individual and the society also fear indiscriminate use of wiretapping or electronic eavesdropping. Many police officials, on the other hand, argue that their only known entrance into organized crime comes through the wiretap.

Evidence gained through *unreasonable* searches and seizures is generally inadmissible in state and federal courts. The *Mapp* v. *Ohio* decision of the U. S. Supreme Court, for example, held that since a crime is a specific violation of law, specific standards for the inclusion or exclusion of evidence from the trial process must also be defined. Earlier decisions restrained the police from creating conditions designed to entrap the violator in the commission of a criminal act. These were followed by judgments which prohibited the use of unconstitutional means to acquire evidence on the ground that the police are not exempt from the standards set for the general public. So that the public could be safeguarded from oppressive police tactics common in a totalitarian police state, the courts formulated an exclusionary rule of evidence, which held that tainted evidence is not objective evidence. The Court in effect questioned the value of justice which convicts a citizen on the basis of illegally seized evidence—a violation in itself.

Although the early application of the exclusionary rule led to the immediate release of several known criminals, the Court assumed that the freedom of law-abiding citizens and the future security of the society could be guaranteed only by the equal application of justice and the elevation of local and state enforcement standards. The use of illegal means to gain evidence for conviction of a citizen who is *innocent* in a court of law until *proved guilty* is, the Court held, a violation of the man's constitutional rights. Since the burden of proof rests with those who accuse the man of crime, they have no right to use illegal means to secure evidence of another's *alleged* illegal acts.

The wiretapping-eavesdropping issue is especially serious because it allows the undetected intrusion of a person's privacy. Since the question of personal privacy cannot be readily separated from concepts of due process, the rights of persons securing them against unreasonable searches and seizures, and constitutional and common law rules excluding tainted evidence from admission in court, the problem poses serious and currently unpredictable consequences. Since modern criminologists recognize that most citizens commit multiple criminal violations each day, the indiscriminate use of wiretapping and eavesdropping devices could readily subject an individual to eventual prosecution. Although the 1968 Crime Control Act allows the use of wiretapping or eavesdropping under court supervision, the argument is far from settled. Since wiretapping implies that one may unknowingly testify against himself, its implications are vast for both the individual and the society.

The American Constitution guarantees the privilege against self-incrimination. But at what point is the person testifying *for* or *against* himself during an overheard and possibly recorded conversation? Also note that tapes of conversations may easily be spliced and copies edited.

Free Press—Fair Trial

The rights of the individual and the rights of the group come into sharp conflict in the issue of free press versus fair trial. The argument centers in the question whether the First Amendment, guaranteeing freedom of the press, is at odds with the Sixth Amendment, maintaining the right to a fair trial. The demand for news following the assassination of President Kennedy, for example, made the question of a fair trial for Lee Harvey Oswald and Jack Ruby academic.

Recognizing that certain news media representatives transgressed the bounds of legitimate news reporting, the Warren Commission, appointed to probe the circumstances surrounding the assassination, later recommended that communications media adopt self-determined standards of conduct. The Press-Bar Committee of the American Society of Newspaper Editors rejected this suggestion, holding that a code would lessen public confidence in news media independence. On the other hand, the press, they argued, has an obligation to ferret out any and all information for publication. While expressing a subtle fear of government and administrative officials, the committee assumed the posture of a watchman over the judicial system.

Opponents of this position argue that each individual person charged with an alleged crime must have the right to protect himself in a court of law. The accusatory process of modern law, they assume, places the burden of proof on the prosecutor, who is limited by time-tested interpretations of rules concerning evidence and procedure. While the Sixth Amendment guarantees the accused a speedy and public trial by an impartial jury, the benefit of the open trial, the opponents hold, is *for* the accused and *not* the press.

The carnival atmosphere of the 1954 trial of Dr. Samuel Sheppard in Cleveland, Ohio, was overcome only by a new trial granted some 12 years later, when the U. S. Supreme Court, by an $8-1$ majority held that trial courts must take strong measures to insure that jury balance is never weighted *in favor* or *against* the accused—since modern communications make an uninformed jury impossible. While the press remains free to report the events that occur in the courtroom, the trial judge must always move to protect the rights of the alleged violator. The new rules devised by Judge Francis J. Talty to augment the Supreme Court decision in the second Sheppard trial were later applied to the case of Richard Speck, convicted murderer of eight student nurses in Chicago.

Members of the American Newspaper Publisher's Association continue to assume that no real conflict exists between the First and Sixth Amendments to the Constitution. Any assumption that pretrial news is intrinsically prejudicial, they argue, is based on conjecture and not on fact. A free press demands not only the freedom to print without restraint but also the free and uninhibited access to information that the public should possess. The restriction or censorship of news, they maintain, carries implied public danger which may even result in eventual secret arrests or clandestine trials. The task of the press, therefore, is to allay public fear and dispel rumor by disclosure of facts, recognizing that some individual rights may be violated in rare or isolated cases. With few exceptions the press, they hold, has maintained its basic responsibility. One of the citizens' basic rights is the right to know. Neither the press nor the bar has the right to bargain this right away.

Although the issues of pretrial and trial publicity

follow separate lines of development, they remain closely allied in principle. The desire to guarantee an impartial jury led the Court to criticize the pretrial publication of confessions or interviews with the accused and/or prospective witnesses, statements of prior criminal record or activity, press discussions of inadmissible evidence, publication of information indicating the failure of the suspect to take a lie detector test or to cooperate with police, pretrial statements by defense counsel concerning the merits of the case, sensationalism in reporting facts or assumptions, and the general titillation of the public before the commencement of a trial. Attempts to neutralize a jury already conditioned by press accounts, the Court noted, are largely impossible and impractical. The advent of television, too, has made the problem even more acute.

The debate regarding free press and fair trial is largely an argument between representatives of the legal profession and the news media. The rights each claim, however, do not belong fully to either group, since both are the rights of citizens and, more specifically, the rights of society. Although the press claims to serve the public interest by disclosing the full facts of each case, its sense of public responsibility has too often been influenced by its competitive need to sell a sensational commodity. In any case, pretrial and trial competition among press reporters, defense lawyers, and prosecuting attorneys hardly serve to guarantee the goal of impartial justice.

The Right to Legal Counsel

Claims that the decisions of the Supreme Court have handcuffed the police reached an early peak following the 1964 *Escobedo* v. *Illinois* decision. The later

June 1966 *Miranda* v. *Arizona* decisions caused even greater bitterness. The Escobedo decision, which held that a person accused of crime could not be denied legal counsel during a police interrogation although no formal charges had been filed against him, as had formerly been common, shook the foundations of modern justice. Since more than 85 percent of all court convictions were based on confessions or guilty pleas, the formal recognition of immediate right to a lawyer challenged existing police and prosecution practice.

The Chicago police refused Danny Escobedo, accused of complicity in the murder of his brother-in-law, legal aid during his second interrogation, although his lawyer, seen by the suspect, stood immediately outside the interrogation room. When trapped into a confession, Escobedo implicated a confederate and later stated that he had offered an accomplice $500 to kill his sister's husband when promised freedom in exchange for a full statement. Although the Illinois Supreme Court at first reversed Escobedo's conviction, holding that the confession was obtained under a false promise of freedom, the court later reinstated the original penalty when the state introduced the detective's denial of promised leniency at a rehearing.

When *Escobedo* v. *Illinois* reached the Supreme Court, the Court moved to eliminate swearing contests between defendants and police interrogators by substituting an *objective* test for confessions. Holding that the accusatory system of justice places the burden of proof on the prosecution, court bias in favor of or against the prosecution undermines court impartiality and encourages biased justice. Since criminal prosecutions actually start in the "squeal room," the Court held that the criminal suspect must have the right to consult legal counsel at this point in the interrogation process. If the defense attorney enters into the case only at the trial stage, the conviction is already academic since a voluntary "confession" undermines the basic constitutional right of the accused to legal defense. Both true and false confession, the Court reasoned, can be coerced through the use of scientific techniques of false sympathy, emotional pressure, threat, or skillful interrogation. Since the accused can make a meaningful waiver of his constitutional right to remain silent only if he knows this right exists, the police, the Court held, must warn the accused of his right to silence. The trial is little more than an appeal from interrogation, the verdict having been rendered in the police station, if counsel is not available to the accused during the critical questioning period.

The 1966 Miranda decision carried the Escobedo judgment several steps further. As a constitutional requisite for admission of a confession in court, the Court stipulated that a suspect must be warned prior to questioning that he has a right to remain silent, that any statement he makes may be used as evidence, and that he possesses the right to engage a self-retained or court-appointed attorney. Although decided by a five-to-four opinion of the Supreme Court, *Miranda* v. *Arizona* was only one of four cases involving similar questions of interrogation and legal representation decided that day. Although Escobedo and Miranda opponents argue that a 5−4 or 6−3 vote does not offer sufficient public support for the judgment, a *Harvard Law Review* study of more than 1,200 opinions of the Supreme Court between 1963 and 1965 revealed that only 34.2% (432) were unanimous opinions. In fact the conservative interpretation which prohibited the general right of all persons, poor and rich, to counsel was maintained in previous years by only a 5 − 4 vote.

Law enforcement spokesmen have led the public to believe that police efforts have been undermined, but the underlying consequences of the Court's action has led the systems of enforcement and justice to adopt more scientific techniques and procedures. Overdependence on a confession as evidence, the Court argued, has actually hindered the development of a reliable enforcement institution and has caused an overemphasis on psychological and physical force to the detriment of respect for law. Since the confession is less reliable than intrinsic evidence secured through skillful investigation, new methods and approaches in enforcement must be developed and utilized.

If the exercise of constitutional rights undermines effective enforcement, law enforcement, the Court reasoned, remains in a sad state. The respect for law can be encouraged only as the public demands and supports the professionalization of the police. As long as public philosophy holds that a man is innocent until proved guilty, the right to an attorney cannot be ignored. Overdependence on easy conviction, the Court theorized, renders enforcement inefficient and subject to mediocrity.

Because the American adversary system of justice depends on the processes of prosecution and defense, the dual procedure of interrogation and debate, demanded in the adversary system, is impossible unless legal counsel is available to the alleged defender at an early stage. If the jury is to serve as the impartial third party to hear the evidence gained through objective police investigation and to decide guilt or innocence, law enforcement must resume its detective and investigative responsibility, leaving criminal prosecution to the district attorney or public prosecutor. Although some criminals may be freed in the early years as enforcement agencies adjust to the new procedures, society should demand an enforcement and judicial system which reflects major advances in human understanding and technological knowledge.

The Rights of Juveniles

The organization of the first juvenile court in Chicago in 1899 offered hope that juveniles would be spared legal retribution and be offered a rehabilitative opportunity at an age when they were still susceptible to positive influences. The juvenile court, however, has neither realized its philosophy nor offered juveniles the constitutional guarantees available to adults. Since juvenile court philosophy and organization assumed that juvenile delinquency is a *civil* and not a criminal act, court procedures in the past were generally exempt from constitutional guarantees surrounding *criminal* prosecution. However, lack of due process allowed hearsay evidence, inadmissible in criminal courts, to serve as the backbone of the juvenile court investigation and "conviction." The right to trial by peers was perverted by the attempt to gain the juvenile's confidence and self-incriminating statement. Although the juvenile court made no formal attempt to judge guilt, it generally assumed guilt by the mere presence of the juvenile in the court.

Before the 1967 Gault decision, the right to counsel at a juvenile court hearing was neither assumed nor encouraged in most jurisdictions. Some judges presumed that the mere presence of a legal representative was indicative of guilt. Others interpreted the presence of a lawyer as a personal threat. Although the Gault decision extends constitutional rights of due process to juvenile court "rehabilitations," most upper- and middle-class youths are able to avoid court contact through early reports of violations to parents rather than police and by the practice of "unofficial probation" without a hearing by the probation officer. Juveniles from lower-class homes are more likely to come under the jurisdiction of the juvenile court.

The advance in civil and legal rights has made the original juvenile-court mandate obsolete. Born of the philosophical tenet that the state is obligated to serve as *parens patriae* and to promote the general welfare, the court has emerged as an agency to protect any child in need. As large numbers of acts, previously handled informally by offending and offended parties, are referred to the court, the scope of jurisdiction has continued to expand. Rather surprisingly, a major volume of court actions are inaugurated by parents against their own children. The existing familial conflict, however, is only further developed by the youth's confrontation with court authoritarianism, reflected in traditional middle-class moral and ethical values which the youth has previously rejected or found to be meaningless in his own environmental situation.

While the juvenile court has emerged as a civil court, its use of power and force to deprive youth of their freedom reveals the court's extracivil character. The fact that 25 percent of all juvenile judges possessed no legal training, that reasonable doubt was not required at juvenile hearings, that commitment was often based on hearsay evidence, that juvenile institutional incarceration often exceeded adult sentences for the same offense, and that 100,000 delinquents were housed in adult jails due to the lack of youth facilities resulted in the promulgation of the 1967 *Gault* v. *Arizona* decision which applied the standards enunciated in the federal case of *Kent* v. *United States* (1966) to the state courts.

The 30- to 90-year prison conviction of Morris Kent, a juvenile accused of housebreaking, robbery, and rape, was reversed by the U. S. Supreme Court in a 5−4 decision on the grounds that the juvenile court judge failed to grant a hearing, to give counsel access to records requested, and to state reasons for his waiver of jurisdiction. The issue was not whether the act was committed; instead, the debate centered on whether the process of justice was fulfilled. Although the juvenile court may have originated for a laudable purpose, there is evidence for concern, the Court noted, that the child neither receives the protection accorded adults nor the solicitous care or regenerative treatment theorized for children. The later Gault decision, however, offered further clarification for the States.

Gerald Gault, a 15-year-old Arizona youth, was judged delinquent and sentenced to a potential 6-year term in the Arizona reformatory for making obscene telephone calls with his friend, son of a Globe (Ariz.) policeman, who was later released without charge. Gault's detention was reported to his parents after a 12-hour lapse, even though a petition filed against him was never served on his parents. Although the complaining woman neither attended the hearing nor testified against the youth, Gault was finally "sentenced" to the State Industrial School (or reformatory) until the age of 21 or until a state board determined his readiness for release to his parents' custody. An Arizona adult committing the same offense would have faced a maximum fine of $50 or 2 months in jail. Gerald Gault served a minimal 6-month term.

When the U. S. Supreme Court reversed Gerald Gault's conviction in 1967, it wrote the contents of the earlier Escobedo and Miranda decisions into juvenile-court philosophy. In a landmark decision the Court held that the rights guaranteed by the Constitution and Bill of Rights applied to the delinquency hearing. Each juvenile, therefore, possessed the right to counsel, whether private or court-appointed, in cases which might result in incarceration; the opportunity to confront and cross-examine witnesses; the privilege against self-incrimination; the right to remain silent; and a guarantee of early notice of charges. Being a boy, the Court argued, "does not justify a kangaroo court." Since society is ever more powerful than any youth, a guarantee of individual rights, the Court noted, is the best guarantee that society, too, will not be subjected to undesirable perversions.

The balance of individual and group rights can only be achieved when the sacredness of every person is balanced with a recognition that each man is one's brother. A framework of self-interest or group coercion benefits but a few and sets the foundation for social unrest and totalitarian response.

Arguments concerning the right to protest unjust laws, to seek security in private conversations, to receive knowledgeable counsel and fair trial, and to guarantee juvenile due process are issues central to the future and must be approached with reason and human understanding.

4
Problems in Law Enforcement

The problems of the American police are compounded by the existence of over 40,000 separate police agencies employing more than 420,000 individuals. Fifty-five of the urban police forces in cities of over 250,000 population employ nearly one third of all police personnel. The cost of policing a city of more than a million persons is $27.31 per resident per year, compared to a cost of $8.74 per resident per year in a city of less than 50,000 persons, estimates the President's Commission. The diversity of police tasks ranging from escorting drunks to apprehending murderers demands a wide variety of abilities, skills, and responses. Enforcement personnel generally see citizens at a time of tension, anger, hatred, fright, violence, drunkenness, or shame — a time when they often overcompensate for their action by righteous indignation or personal attack. A routine police contact, therefore, can readily affect a person's sense of self-respect, dignity, privacy, or personal rights. And yet the police are charged with the duty to protect the community, act as diplomats, and remain physically and emotionally stable.

Modern policemen are trained to apprehend and prosecute criminals. Additional training which might lead the officer to safeguard community security by minimizing group frustration or other social threat has been largely ignored. Most police are trained to perform such routine procedures as searching a person or house for weapons, transporting a suspect to the police station, taking fingerprints, writing arrest reports, and testifying in court, but they have received limited training, if any, in dealing with situations involving human interaction. An overdependence on power and coercion has resulted in a negative police image, especially among the lower classes. Some recent riots were touched off by commonplace citizen-police street encounters. Paradoxically, the riots occurred in high-crime areas where enforcement is least effective and policemen are looked on with suspicion. The need for the policeman to be the agent for the *whole* society can no longer be ignored.

Police and Community Tensions

The police image is at a new low. Although large segments of American society distrust the law enforcement officer, members of minority groups are more likely to show distrust than members of the majority. While 23 percent of the majority whites, for example, felt in 1965 – 66 that the police were doing an excellent job, only 15 percent of nonwhites supported this position. Although 7 percent of whites, the National Opinion Research Center found, believed that the police were doing a poor job, 16 percent of the nonwhite sample held this viewpoint. Sixty-three percent of the whites surveyed held that the police were almost all honest; only 30 percent of the nonwhite community, however, accepted the same viewpoint. While one percent of the white population held that police were almost all corrupt, 10 percent of the nonwhite population accepted this interpretation. Since the police most often represent the community power structure, they become immediate targets for those living in the frustrations of the ghetto. Although most policemen do not discriminate against minority citizens, many contribute to feelings of inferiority by their indifference to minority group aspirations, attitudes, and customs.

Community tensions, however, are not the only problems of the modern enforcement officer. Specialized skills have become prerequisites for successful urban enforcement. However, detective caseloads far exceed the level for effective investigative work. So modern police focus on quick and speedy investigation of those crimes which offer the greatest social threat. While crimes against the person (murder, aggravated assault, and rape) receive immediate attention, reports of theft or burglary are often ignored. And many crimes are never reported to the police because the public believes that the police are ineffective. Professional, organized, or neophyte criminals probably share this conviction and therefore find crime rewarding.

New Technology and Law Enforcement

The time lapse between a call for help and the patrol response largely determines whether the offender will be apprehended. This means that effective enforcement ultimately depends on qualified officers and adequate police administration. A Los Angeles study revealed that arrests were completed if the average response time was less than 4.1 minutes; arrests, however, were not made when the average response was 6.3 minutes. Nearly 36 percent of all arrests in Los Angeles during January 1966 were made within half an hour after the commission of the crime. Crime control in metropolitan Chicago, on the other hand, was hindered until the early 1960s by the mere fact that only three telephone trunk lines were available to police headquarters for the whole city of Chicago. Before the new police superintendent, Orlando Wilson, assumed office, the time lapse between a crime report and a patrol response often ranged as high as 30 to 45 minutes.

Modern technology has stimulated some new police procedures, but the need for more street patrolmen, whether on foot or motorized, continues. Nearly 62 percent of more than 9,000 major crimes against the person committed in Chicago over a 6-month period occurred on the streets or at other public premises. Subway crimes in New York City, however, declined by 36 percent in 1966 after uniformed transit patrolmen were assigned to every late-night train. Although the principal purpose of patrol is to deter crime, the most effective urban deterrent methods are still unknown.

Many argue that the return of beat patrolmen would reestablish police-community relationships, but the higher costs have negated this proposal. Patrolmen in cruising automobiles can cover more territory at lower costs. The automobile allows greater police mobility and also serves as a means of transport in emergencies or at times of arrest. Since most police departments are understaffed, few can afford the luxury of patrolmen on foot. Even patrol deterrence, however, is not likely to affect crimes of emotion and hate (for example, murder and aggravated assault). Although the ratio of policemen to residents may vary from 1.07 to 4.04 per thousand residents, no exact correlation can be established between the police-citizen ratios and crime rates.

The Policeman and Social Problems

The modern policeman fulfills many tasks not directly identifiable with crime detection or offender apprehension. Traffic control, automobile inspection, public operations, and community service have become identified with local police operations, but they take large amounts of time away from crime control. The trivial duties associated with modern police functions compound the problem of detection and law enforcement.

Since the police function is more than one of enforcement and apprehension, the future police force must serve multiple functions. The single-track enforcement system must give way, the President's Commission concluded, to a triple-access system which would allow better qualified officers to assume responsibilities commensurate with their education without having to serve long apprenticeship in the ranks. The *community service officer*, trained to observe community happenings and to mobilize community agencies for the correction of local deficiencies before full-scale crime develops, represents the lowest police rank. His task entails giving community services to which citizens are entitled. Although the community service officer would necessarily assume a broadened police function, the redefinition of police roles might, the President's Commission believed, enhance community respect for and sense of identity with the police. Since housing, parks, welfare, and health are related to the crime problem, communities should create municipal planning boards which bring together local police, community planning, and other urban experts. Joint cooperation by police, community, city planning, and other urban experts is ultimately necessary if community reintegration is to be accomplished.

Officers Must Possess Special Skills

The need for officer training in community and minority problems has become obvious. The complexity of the modern urban life has complicated enforcement functions. The subtle difference between the control of crime and coercion of minority members (often assumed by the police to commit the most crime) and the joint cooperation of the community to uphold the law must be recognized if respect for law, order, and the police is to be established and maintained. The encouragement of minority members to participate in police functions is only the first step to a changed police-ghetto and ghetto-police relationship.

Riot prevention programs offer the best means of controlling this form of antisocial disorder. Riots are expressions of abnormal behavior arising from abnormal situations. Because the tactics used at the beginning of any disorder are crucial to eventual riot control, police and National Guard training and advance planning are important to contain the problem.

Containment, however, merely treats the symptom, not the disease. Riots arise from imaginary or real situations in the rioter's experience. Intelligence resources are needed to gain understanding of community problems long before disorders develop.

The major increase in new laws, the demand for sophisticated legal understanding, and the complexity of modern social problems require qualified and well-educated policemen. The new policeman needs to identify with people and to be sensitive to community needs. The community must come to view him as a reflection of itself. Since the best enforcement is enforcement voluntarily given, it can best be achieved when the community and the police work in a concerted manner toward known goals. The recruitment of minority members for the police function, therefore, assumes great importance. Arbitrary height restrictions which exclude shorter Puerto Ricans from police employment automatically eliminate many potentially valuable officers in minority areas. Minimal salary scales, conceived in the attempt to keep taxes down, only serve to encourage mediocrity and enhance police frustration. The community needs to ask what kind of enforcement it can expect when police officers must work at a second job to earn a living.

Although increased education must be demanded in the future, present entry standards for enforcement jobs limit nonwhite male participation. A sample 1966 census reported that 78 percent of all white males between the ages of 20 and 24 had completed 4 years of high school, but only 53 percent of nonwhite males had reached the same level. Since qualifications differ, police departments might allow several points of entry into the enforcement process rather than demand that each officer begin as a rookie and work up through the ranks. Most cities are already 10 percent below authorized police strength because of the lack of successful police candidates evaluated against minimal entrance standards. Only 3 percent of all 1965 applicants were able to meet the rigorous standards of the Los Angeles police department. While applicant success rates have declined, retirement rates are beginning to increase. Forty-one percent of the Los Angeles police force alone was eligible for retirement in 1967. Fifty thousand new policemen are already needed to bring all departments to authorized strength.

The Problem of Multiple Police Systems

The multiplicity of separate police agencies has complicated the problem of law enforcement. Sixty-three percent of the American population (113 million persons) resided in 212 Standard Metropolitan Statistical Areas in 1960. The 212 metropolitan areas encompassed 313 counties and 4,144 cities, each marked by its own police force. Since most local departments were small and possessed limited service facilities, their ability to deal with large-scale criminal activity was severely limited. Often overzealous in their independence, they have failed in the past to coordinate or pool their enforcement potential in order to offer modern coherent enforcement services to major metropolitan areas. Since pooling may involve the consolidation or merger of one or more police jurisdictions, effective territorial enforcement (often more effective since it minimizes jurisdictional questions) depends on the goodwill of the participating communities. However, this approach is only a stopgap measure.

Personnel, planning, records, and communications systems should be developed on a statewide basis. The problem of crime can be attacked only by full-scale local, state, and federal cooperation. Multiple city or county agencies to investigate vice, organized crime, or fugitive escapees can be created only through joint participation and coordination. Economies of scale allow large departments to provide trained investigators to smaller enforcement agencies only for specialized police investigations. In the contemporary setting the need is to augment local jurisdiction while protecting the right of local enforcement. Mutual aid agreements allowing interdepartmental borrowing between police departments in times of disaster, public events, riots, and civil disorders offer new hope for continued police security and service. Although metropolitan government (Metro) offers an ultimate political base for consolidation of urban governments, the vested interests of local communities has restricted any large movement toward the adoption of this form of political reorganization.

Multiple investigation of the same crime, encouraged by the fragmentation of patrol and investigative forces, can best be overcome by the development of team policing. Under this approach, all police work, whether patrol or criminal investigation, would be unified under a specific command. The police agents, police officers, and community service officers, members of a team, would meet at the beginning of the duty tour to receive a briefing on the current neighborhood situation from a field supervisor, who would assign each team to specific city blocks to carry out delegated duties. Under this procedure flexible enforcement patterns could be shaped daily to the needs of the community rather than be tied to inflexible manpower commitments. While narcotics or juvenile officers could continue their specialized duties, they could cover specific or wider territories as the need arose. Although team policing would demand a redistribution and reorganization of present personnel, it offers, the President's Crime Commission believed, the potential for increased crime solution and more advantageous use of police energies.

Team policing can become possible only as adequate administrative procedures are placed in effect. Urban police systems, however, have failed to develop career administrators to activate the police process. Police organization generally fails to reflect recognized management and organizational principles. Until urban police departments are modernized, reorganized, and redirected to new management techniques, effective law enforcement will continue to remain a hope rather than a reality. Effective personnel deployment demands an overarching enforcement design, which in turn depends upon effective management operation. Police professionalization cannot be achieved by neighborhood control through local politicians. Since the best patrolman must depend on strong staff services, his work cannot be maximized without departmental specialists. Long-range police administration, therefore, must supersede day-to-day or crisis-to-crisis enforcement planning.

Research and analysis concerning short- and long-range crime trends can offer objective insight into crime-encouraging social conditions. Plans developed to control problems of urban disorganization can only be effected by creative planning. Enforcement paralysis, evident at the time of the ghetto riots, illustrates the problem. The need to provide useful liaison among police officers, prosecutors, community representatives, legal experts, moral leaders, and other influential community members is now apparent.

Police enforcement, however, can only be as good as police integrity. Strong internal investigation units must guarantee police incorruptibility. Public disrespect for the police, often encouraged by police corruption, undermines law enforcement. Since much of the reported police rudeness, disrespect, and "police brutality" occur in ghetto areas, nonwhite officers should be assigned to internal investigation units charged with the power to detect, investigate, and report violating officers and to deter police criminality by identifying problem areas or situations which might encourage police misconduct. The internal investigation unit is most effective when it is directly responsible to the chief of police.

Because the policeman ultimately determines who is arrested or released, he assumes an awesome responsibility for the public good and potential citizen harm. The enforcement function has become too complex to allow the continuance of psychologically disturbed, incompetent, or unqualified personnel in sensitive police positions.

Christian citizens have a deep concern that qualified men be appointed and that they do their work effectively.

5
The System of Justice

The majority of criminal violations are never prosecuted. Not only do policemen utilize their vast discretionary power by failing to arrest particular offenders, but prosecutors further dilute the process by failing to prosecute all violators brought to their attention. Nearly 90 percent of all cases coming before the court are disposed of by guilty pleas. The system of criminal justice, however, cannot operate without administrative shrinkage in the prosecution process. If all arrests resulted in prosecution, the courts would be immobilized for years to come. While the guilty plea often undermines the search for true justice, it has emerged as an expedient measure to guarantee quick court processing of criminal charges. If all laws were equally enforced, the courts would not only be clogged, but society would also be thoroughly repressed.

The Alleged Violator and Due Process

In the American system the criminal court is limited to the prosecution and judgment of specific violations of particular legal codes. Since criminal penalties can be invoked only against those proved to be in violation of particular statutes, the court is prohibited from imposing sanctions against a person who merely anticipates or is thought to intend a given act, except in cases where conspiracy is prohibited by law.

The concept of due process, derived from English common law, demands that a defendant be formally notified of the charge against him, have opportunity to confront witnesses, be able to present evidence in his own behalf, and have a jury of peers able to interpret the evidence against the backdrop of social attitudes and practice. More recent extensions of due-process concepts have incorporated the right of the defendant to representation by an attorney at any probationary hearing, interrogation, or court action.

Since the law values *due* process over *efficient* process, it recognizes that to protect the innocent a percentage of criminals may go free. Under American due-process procedures no man can be required by court order or subpoena to produce papers against himself. Search warrants, too, may be used only to seize items directly pertaining to the crime; under modern rules of evidence, illegally seized evidence is not admissible in court.

Criminal law is impersonal and fails to consider the behavioral differences between a theft motivated by personal hunger and a larceny stimulated by desire to obtain someone else's property. Dangerous and harmful acts against the person, evidenced in homicide, rape, assault, and robbery, are universally abhorred. The greater volume of criminal cases, however, involves consistent violations of general social norms or problems of drunkenness, disorderly conduct, vagrancy, gambling, or minor sexual violations with willing victim cooperation.

Under present statues the state attempts to act as the conscience and constraint of the person. Police activity and court calendars, as a result, are burdened with large numbers of minor offenders who are summarily treated with treadmill justice while more serious crime continues uncontrolled. Even now current court procedures allow any community to ignore the social problems of the alcoholic, the compulsive gambler, the homeless man, and the psychologically aberrant sexual deviant. Since mere imprisonment fails to reach the core of these problems, eventual release usually occurs without significant changes in attitudes and behavior.

From Rural to Urban

Part of the modern-day problem in adjudication is the rural-oriented court system. Designed originally for small rural communities, the system has remained inadequate for the emerging urban mass society. Since about two thirds of all American counties are predominantly rural, urban needs are being met slowly. The former close community relationship between all principals in the rural criminal case has been replaced by a sense of impersonality in the urban court. The press of the court calendar and the tensions caused by inadequate staff often result in judicial decisions based on limited evidence and ineffective investigations.

In its own way the diversity of urban life breeds a lack of public concern and understanding. Variations in social class, attitudes, dress, speech, and manners affect the disposition of the case. The volume of court cases has caused shortcuts and overloads which have undermined an effective urban system of justice. The practice of bargaining and pleading guilty to a lesser sentence to avoid costs of court trial and to gain a lesser sentence has become so commonplace that the theoretical principles of modern justice have been threatened. While guilty pleas accounted for nearly 90 percent of all past convictions, the trial of the remaining cases did not automatically result in successful prosecutions—an indication that justice in court may be somewhat different from the bargained justice of the prosecuting attorney and the defendant's lawyer.

Crisis in the Lower Criminal Courts

The problem of justice is especially acute in the lower criminal courts where poorly trained personnel, lack of decorum, and perfunctory adherence to concepts of legal justice have levied their toll on the first offender. The fundamental principles of true justice have often been lost in the desire to dispose quickly of "less serious" cases in a few minutes. Four judges in the District of Columbia Court of General Sessions, for example, processed more than 1,500 felony cases, 7,500 serious misdemeanors, 38,000 petty offenses, and additional traffic offenses in a 1-year period. Since these judges heard cases during a daily 3- to 5-hour period, the time given to "justice" was less than a 40-hour week.

Justice conceived in haste may often be no justice at all. The frustrations of the lower courts eventually touch all participants in the judicial process. Any system of courts that threatens defendants charged with minor offenses with less dignity and courtesy than persons charged with serious crimes cannot be justified. The President's Commission recommended that the lower criminal court be unified and standardized in order to provide adequate services.

The justice of the peace court, a rural expression of the lower criminal court, is likewise deficient. Since the compensation of the justice is fixed by a fee assessed against the parties involved in the particular case, the system is open to perversion and kickbacks. The court continues to exist in 35 states; the justices of the peace are not required to be lawyers in more than 30 states.

The need to revise the justice of the peace system is well documented. All criminal cases, the Commission noted, should be tried by judges of equal status under generally comparable procedures.

Justice Is Not Without Delay

While many state and the federal constitutions prescribe that any alleged offender must appear in court without unnecessary delay, the lapse of time between the preliminary hearing and the grand jury action may be 3 months or more in some jurisdictions. Persons charged with serious crimes may often wait a year or more for trial. In such instances elementary concepts of fairness to both the defendant and the community are ignored. Not only is the defendant placed in a position of "serving time" while awaiting the trial, but if released on bail, he may actually circumvent justice by forcing witness inconvenience, trial continuance, or misadministration of the system of justice. Effective court management, of course, can overcome these limitations. However, since the judge traditionally controls the court calendar, effective management may fall victim to the large number of cases coming before his jurisdiction.

By comparison, English justice is swift. Arrest, trial, and appeal take less than 4 months in England. American criminal justice may be long and frustrating. The prosecution, judgment, and appeal processes alone may consume several years, since American courts often represent both state and federal interests. Although felony cases could be decided within a 4-month period (an appeal of conviction adding another 5 months), current methods do not generally allow such quick case disposition except in smaller jurisdictions with fewer criminal cases.

Proposed Changes in the System of Justice

The application of computer-programming techniques to the court calendar has rarely been attempted in the United States, although it offers hope for the future. However the courts have been dominated by principles enunciated for a rural community and have failed to keep pace with the needs and demands of an urban nation. Only through the application of management techniques and the use of business machines can court process and procedures be modernized. Even clerical methods must be reformed. The central supervision of judges alone would make it possible to assign judges more judiciously, to vary work and vacation schedules, and to gain greater efficiency from judges of lesser personal competence. While court reorganization could bring this end in sight, the problem of the defendant continues.

Although more than one half of all defendants brought before the magistrate court (lower court) are released or sentenced within 24 hours after their arrest, the cases of the remaining alleged offenders are finally processed during a several-month period, depending on the seriousness of the case, the prosecutor's case load, and the volume of cases on the court calendar. If the court is unable to hear the case quickly, the defendant may find himself in continued custody unless he is able to post bond.

The bail system, however, discriminates against the poor and violates the basic principles of equal justice for all defendants. Twenty-five percent of all persons arrested in New York during a period of one recent study, for example, were unable to furnish the necessary money (5 to 10 percent of the bond desired) to engage a bondsman to post a $500 bond. Forty-five percent failed at a $1,500 bond, while 63 percent failed at $2,500. Inability to post bond caused their temporary incarceration in a local or county jail at taxpayer expense. In addition, they were unable to work at jobs where they might have gained enough income to post adequate bond.

Since most jurisdictions spend $3 to $9 per day to house, feed, and guard a jail defendant, it would be less expensive and more valuable to allow the release of minor offenders on their own recognizance as encouraged by the Vera Institute of Justice. Vera studies revealed that prisoners unable to post bond were more often convicted than those able to make bail. These discoveries encouraged the passage of the Federal Bail Reform Act of 1966, which authorizes judges to place nonmonetary conditions on the defendant's release, whether in the form of assigning the defendant to another person or organization, restricting his travel, or placing him in partial custody so that he might continue outside employment during the day and be confined at night.

The Quest for Qualified Judges

The system of justice ultimately depends on the quality of the judiciary. Although many methods are currently employed to select judges, appointment of qualified men is more desirable than public election of judicial officials. Appointment, however, should be based on a representative selection system which insures the high quality of potential candidates for the office. Long tenure with fixed retirement ages serves to insulate the judge from undue political influence. Since approximately one half of all newly selected judges possess no prior courtroom experience, continuing training and in-service retraining programs for the judiciary are necessary. Because the average judge serves some 25 years before retirement, early development of judicial criteria and standards have special importance. A California commission charged with the examination of judicial conduct and the recommendation of appropriate action stimulated numerous retirements or resignations and the removal of 26 judges in a 4-year period.

The Search for Competent Prosecutors

The maintenance of high standards in criminal prosecution is equally critical. Since the prosecutor ultimately determines which cases will be or will not be prosecuted, his position is pivotal to the whole system of criminal justice. Although the prosecutor, with the possible exception of the judge, is the most important officer in the courtroom drama, many prosecutors are only part-time officers of the court, elected for relatively short terms through partisan political elections. They are often underpaid, and many engage in private law practice, a procedure which may lead to periodic conflicts of interest or other community tensions. Although the election of the prosecutor insures that law enforcement and prosecution will remain under community control, the need to provide an independent prosecution power base is different. Since most prosecutors simply embark upon their office without previous experience, special prosecutor training programs are necessary. State and national prosecution practice must be standardized. Modern mobile society demands a more coherent system of prosecution and justice.

The Need for Capable Defense Attorneys

The growing complexity of modern justice has made the availability of defense counsel to all defendants mandatory. The *Gideon* v. *Wainright* and *Miranda*

v. *Arizona* decisions of the U. S. Supreme Court have prescribed that defense counsel must be available to all arrested persons if the results of the police questioning are to be later admitted as evidence in court. Although the increased use of counsel may complicate the process of justice, its availability may guarantee the defendant's right to due process. Only defense counsel, for example, knows when evidence is admissible in court and is able to challenge its validity. Since the system of justice, like the system of government, depends on a system of checks and balances, the negation of the role of defense counsel can only undermine the total configuration of American justice. Although the greater use of defense lawyers will result in increased costs, delays, and fewer convictions, only their presence can guarantee the right to due process for the benefit of society.

Standardization of Criminal Law Codes

American justice is complicated by inconsistent laws and sentencing codes. Since laws are created in response to public need, they often reflect current sentiment rather than contemporary knowledge. The more than 1,413 offenses contained in the Oregon penal code have 466 variable penalties. Colorado statutes, the President's Commission reported, inconsistently requires that an offender convicted of first-degree murder serve a minimum of 10 years before becoming eligible for parole, while a person convicted of a lesser degree of murder must serve 15 or more years before consideration. Killing a dog in one state carries a maximum of 6 months imprisonment, but stealing a dog is punishable by 10 years in prison.

Although armed bank robbery under federal law is punishable by fines, probation, or sentence up to 25 years, armed robbery of a post office under federal law specifies either probation or the imposition of a 25-year prison sentence. The lack of alternatives often causes a sentencing judge to grant probation rather than impose a mandatory high sentence.

Although nearly one half of the States are now revising their penal laws and sentencing codes, the task to be completed remains monumental. The Model Penal Code of the American Law Institute divides all crimes into three felony grades and two misdemeanor levels. Each grade carries a maximum penalty in cases of special seriousness and the discretion to grant probation except in capital cases. Under its provisions judges would be given authority to impose flexible sentences, taking the context of a particular case into consideration.

To maximize the value of the parole process, parole boards would similarly be given power to review the sentence soon after the convicted offender entered the correctional process.

The Modern Penal Code also suggests the definition of sentencing criteria which could be used by the judge in determining the actual sentence imposed. Under its provisions the offender's sentence would be determined in relation to the seriousness of the offense, the need for treatment, and the potential threat the offender posed to society. Eleven grounds for granting probation would include the relative mildness of the offense, the character of the offender, and the hardships that imprisonment would impose on the offender or his family. The proposed revisions attempt to differentiate the situational offender from the persistent, hardened, or habitual criminal.

Revision of Sentencing Procedures

Sentencing procedures need revision. Not only should all court jurisdictions, whether misdemeanor or felony, provide probation services, but jury sentencing in noncapital cases should also be abolished. Presentence reports should be available to the defendant and his counsel unless compelling reasons for nondisclosure exist. If the rehabilitation of the offender is the ultimate goal, all segments of the court process should work collectively to that end. In too many cases, however, the goal of justice is merely successful prosecution or successful defense without major concern for the eventual rehabilitation of the offender. The need continues for acquainting judges, probation officers, and prosecuting and defense attorneys with the problems of incarceration and rehabilitation.

The modern attempt to reduce disparity in sentencing has resulted in the development of sentencing councils and the appellate review of sentences. The sentencing council, consisting of several judges who meet periodically to discuss alternative penalties, works to formulate common sentencing practices for consideration by the sentencing judge, who retains ultimate responsibility for pronouncing judgment. The appellate review of sentences, on the other hand, refers to the systematic and continuous examination of specific sentences and policy in an appeals court. To date twelve states and Congress, in cases of military courts, have granted authority for appellate review in the attempt to overcome the wide disparity in state sentencing practices. These are only first steps toward a thorough revision of the court system.

The Christian and the System of Justice

The general public quickly loses interest in the problem of the offender and his offense after arrest and conviction. The quality of the courts and the system of correction remains a continuing concern for the Christian. His Christian vocation as a servant of God in the world includes working for a fair system of justice and for rehabilitation of the offender. Christians can exert their influence in organizations designed to evaluate the situation and work for court revisions.

6

Society's Response to Crime and the Criminal

The public attitude toward crime is filled with paradoxes. It is concerned about "crime in the streets," but it remains unwilling to raise taxes to pay police a living wage, to add necessary personnel, or to equip its officers. Although arguing that the courts have hamstrung the law-enforcement effort, it ignores the fact that more than 75 percent of the property crimes reported to the police never result in *any* police arrest. Even though the public demands an end to violence, in the name of individual freedom it resists laws requiring gun registration. As a citizen a father may demand quick arrest and processing of juvenile offenders, but as a father he may seek special exemption for his own child.

Most citizens are self-righteous and indignant concerning crime. Believing that they are law-abiding citizens, they quickly condemn the alleged offender, at the same time ignoring his context or condition. Crime is something that few, especially those in the suburbs, directly experience. Consequently they are content to cry for harsh punishment without concern for its end results. Almost instinctively, the public feels satisfaction with an order to shoot to kill but accepts no responsibility for the need to rehabilitate and remotivate.

Most persons seek easy answers to complex problems. The average father is unconcerned until his daughter is raped. The general businessman is slow to support an enlarged police force until his store is robbed or burglarized. The church member may show little concern for the educational program of his community until the dropout problem threatens the community. Because of indifference and neglect, society no doubt deserves its present inefficient system of laws, law enforcement, and correction.

The Response Is Uneven

The public no longer believes that criminals possess evil spirits which must be exorcised by corporal punishment or death. Some may still believe that punishment by imprisonment will remotivate the offender regardless of his ability to earn a living. The public often does not realize that prison dehumanizes the inmate as it restricts his work opportunities, depersonalizes his individual relationships in an institutional setting, and broadens his knowledge of criminal skills and procedures. The impersonality of prison dress, limited visiting and letterwriting privileges, restrictions on conversation, the double-file marching system, and the characteristic inmate culture undermine the long-range correctional goals of the modern penal institution.

Recent attempts have been made to change correctional philosophy from letting the punishment fit the crime to a principle of fitting the treatment to the needs of the individual offender, but correctional systems are largely unable to adapt to this concept. Penal philosophy may have passed beyond the point of attributing delinquent-criminal behavior to demons or defective psychological character, but only in recent years have correctional theorists come to understand that crime and delinquency also reflect the conditions of social disorganization, individual maladjustment, and ambiguous socioethical values which give opportunity and impetus to innate tendencies.

Correctional Goals

Four goals, attempted simultaneously and often in conflict with each other, are involved in the correctional process.

The goal of *custody* or *isolation* is to separate the offender from the "normal" community. The philosophy of punishment assumes that the pleasure inherent in crime can be eliminated through infliction of pain or deprivation of pleasure.

The philosophy of *deterrence*, closely related to the idea of punishment, presumes that harsh punishments inflicted on the offender will discourage other potential juvenile or criminal offenders.

The *rehabilitative* goal is to redirect existing behavior patterns in the attempt to redefine and reorient personal conduct and values. The systems of correction and treatment are dominated by concern for custody of the offender.

First and foremost, prison officials attempt to guarantee the security of the community through isolation of the prisoner from the broader "noncriminal" society. The excessive cost of isolation leaves limited resources for long-term rehabilitative planning and treatment. On the other hand, supervision of the offender through *probation* (community release under the supervision of the probation officer without sentence to prison) and *parole* (release from prison for good behavior under the supervision of a parole officer before completion of the maximum sentence) not only offer greater rehabilitation potential but also cost less.

Limitations of the Prison

The prison fails to treat the central causes which stimulated the original delinquent or criminal activity or gave opportunity for delinquency. Many delinquents and criminals are disturbed or frustrated youth. Others are alcoholics, narcotic addicts, senile offenders, or sex deviants who have differing problems and can only be treated in specialized programs. Most, however, are failures in a culture that does not allow for failure. Many are unable to compete in a society which demands competition. And yet they manage to commit crime and delinquent acts which do not demand particular skill or specialized training and thus compete in their own way.

Their problems are extensive and are not readily solved by a simple jail lockup or penal incarceration. Theirs are problems of life, values, self-concept, ultimate goals, and social alienation. Having either rejected or been rejected by their peers, schools, community, church, employers, and often by their own parents, they are products of abuse, hatred, violence, and hopelessness. Delinquents and criminal offenders find a measure of security, however, among fellow deviants who share a similar problem, social antagonism, and sense of not belonging.

The Public's Attitude to Corrections

American society has often followed the general maxim that "ignorance is bliss" in dealing with the correctional problem. The failure of corrections, however, can no longer be neglected and must be squarely faced in our generation. On any given day the system is responsible for approximately 1.3 million offenders from a total U. S. population of more than 200 million. Nearly 2.5 million admissions and $1 billion are handled yearly in the correctional system. Some of the modern crime increase results from the failure of the correctional system to rehabilitate deviant offenders. The situation is often similar to that found in 1966 in an Indiana prison. Metalworking equipment had remained largely unused because the state legislature was unwilling to appropriate money to hire supervisory personnel. The costs of supervision would have been minimal when compared with the costs of the burning and rioting which ensued after an inmate was severely injured on one of the machines while working without adequate training or supervision.

The correctional system is faced with many handicaps. One of them is the makeup of prison society, in which repeaters and habitual criminals pass on knowledge, attitudes, and techniques to less initiated inmates during imprisonment. Thus the institution remains a paradoxical operation in that it often places a marginal criminal into a greater concentration of known criminality than would normally obtain if he were treated in his own neighborhood. Yet a parolee, who for the time being has been released from a densely criminal prison population, may be returned to prison for parole violation if discovered associating with known criminals.

The Search for a New Direction

The need for a major breakthrough in the correctional approach is evident; modern correction, however, has been dominated by prison architecture rather than by concepts of individual treatment and rehabilitation.

Rising costs and increasing evidence that the prison is largely unsuccessful in any goal other than the isolation of criminals from "good citizens" have prompted experimental attempts to overcome its deficiencies.

The large increase in juvenile delinquency, often a first step towards adult crime, suggests that present correctional weaknesses will only be exaggerated in the next few years if current crime and sentencing trends continue. The failure to distinguish between high- and low-risk offenders has led to incarceration of many persons who would be better served and treated in their own communities. Legislative overdependence on prison sentences as a means of bringing about behavioral changes and controlling crime has continued to expand the prison population during a period of major population growth. As long as legislative and correctional thinking is directed toward the 10 to 15 percent of the incorrigible offender population, the remaining 85 to 90 percent are being exposed to greater criminality, bitterness, and ambiguous correctional goals in the prison setting.

Mere Custody Is Not the Answer

The special problems of disturbed juveniles, chronic alcoholics, narcotic addicts, senile thieves, and sex deviants are not solved by prison sentences. Since the prison emphasizes primarily custody of the offender to protect society from a potential second attack, few lasting changes in behavior result from modern imprisonment. This product of Anglo-Saxon practice and individualistic philosophy fails to meet the challenge of our urban age. In its aim to be economically self-sufficient, the prison too often teaches the convict skills which are unusable outside prison (for example, license-plate manufacturing and farm operations). Because of few work opportunities, many prisoners merely serve time without constructive change or training.

Society is hardly safe, except in its ignorance, if no new goals and attitudes have come to the incarcerated criminal during his imprisonment. Few persons realize that the increase in crime and even ghetto rioting have been directly stimulated by antisocial attitudes developed in the community and reinforced by failures of the judicial and correctional systems.

Local and county jails (where first-time offenders are usually incarcerated) offer minimal facilities and often combine juveniles, women, and first offenders with violent criminals, drunks, and mental defectives. Sexual attacks of prisoners against first offenders, reported in 1967 at the Cook County (Ill.) jail, are more common than enforcement officials will admit. Few misdemeanant institutions provide rehabilitative programs of any type, since these institutions are looked upon as transitional units to the larger prison system.

Treatment of first offenders, however, has been neglected at the expense of future crime. Although early detection and treatment offer the best possibility of crime correction, modern police and correctional systems provide few opportunities for this form of crime control. The lack of coordination between local jails, misdemeanant institutions, and state correctional operations is only an extension of incoherent state and national correctional policy. Ninety-three percent of the American juvenile court jurisdictions, representing 44 percent of the population, provide no juvenile pretrial-detention facilities. In 1965 approximately 100,000 juveniles were confined in adult institutions—either police lockup or county jail.

Of the more than 121,000 persons who worked in American correctional institutions in 1965, 80 percent carried out custodial and maintenance functions. Only 24,000, 20 percent of the staff, worked in probation and parole areas as educators, social workers, psychologists, or psychiatrists. Working with impossible case loads, rehabilitative workers received little relief and merely serviced those they were originally employed to reintegrate and rehabilitate.

Although we stand on the threshold of exciting changes, modern correction is still dominated by the 18th-century emphasis on punishment. Often based on the assumption that each criminal chooses to violate the law because it gives him pleasure or profit, contemporary state correctional policy, although slowly changing, still presumes that stark prison conditions and regimental prison life in which pleasure and profit are absent are the best means of crime control. Originating from the quasi-religious and humanitarian idea that a prisoner will mend his ways if given opportunity to reflect on his own conduct, prison design became an attempt to provide the isolation believed necessary for individual remotivation. Prison attitudes even today encourage each prisoner to do "his own time" without close or meaningful contacts with staff members or other inmates. Prison-inmate culture and informal leadership systems further undermine the rehabilitation potential of the prison.

Staff members are often unable to cope with problems of coerced homosexuality, rackets, violence, corruption, or other inmate abuses. Prison architecture and restrictive legislative enactments have made rehabilitation difficult if not impossible. The rural isolation of the prisoner has merely served to further segregate the urban offender from the society to which he should ultimately adjust. The prison farm illustrates the special paradox of modern corrections. Although prisoners are encouraged to "do constructive time" to reach the privileged sanctuary of the prison farm, they move to a protected community unlike the community from which they have come and to which they will return. Individualized treatment programs for offenders, while increasingly recognized as beneficial, are being only slowly adopted. Failure to see the relationships of individual and society in crime causation has led to wholly inadequate rehabilitation routines. The way to reconcile the individual to his work, school, religion, family, or other activities remains largely unexplored.

Prisons Create Family Strains
and Employment Marginality

While family loyalty and employment opportunity offer the basic foundation for future parole success, major strains are placed on both by imprisonment. Long separations often cause marital conflict and may remove the father from contact with his children at a critical period in their lives. Although some may argue that having a criminal for a father is no positive value, they argue in ignorance. Criminals, like most other people, reflect both deviant and normal attitudes and still serve as important father images for their children. The present correctional system tends to penalize whole families for the act of the single offender, causing family disruptions which only strong family commitment can overcome.

The rapid change of modern society forces a marginal person sentenced to several years in prison into even worse economic position and reduces his potential for future economic success. Also in this respect the current correctional system is generally miscast and inadequate. Men who have already failed are introduced to a system which enhances failure. As long as many members of society believe that adoption of modern correctional methods means coddling evil men, continued increase in crime is not only predictable but *guaranteed*.

The majority of offenders are males between the ages of 16 and 30. Although 55 percent of the inmate population completed 1 to 8 years of elementary school, only 34 percent of the general population was in that category. Another 40 percent of the offender group completed 1 to 4 years of high school, but little more than 5 percent of the inmate population completed one or more years of college. In contrast, nearly 49 percent of the general population completed high school, and 17.8 percent completed 1 to 4 years of college.

The modest educational training of prison inmates is reflected also in their occupational experience. While in 1965 nearly 69 percent of confined inmates had formerly worked as laborers, service workers, or general operatives, primarily unskilled or lower class occupational positions, less than 39 percent of the general labor force were engaged in these occupations. On the other hand, nearly 40 percent of the general labor force worked in clerical and sales, managerial, owner, or professional and technical worker categories. Less than 14 percent of the prison population evidenced work experience in these areas.

Since the prisons attempt to deal with all inmates regardless of social class or occupational experience, they have been given the unenviable task of reconciling and retraining large numbers of already marginal persons. But their high costs and general inefficiency in such rehabilitation make them a modern luxury. Most surprising is the revelation that the average yearly juvenile supervision cost is $328 in the community and $3,613 in an institutional correctional system. While an average adult felony offender may be supervised for $198 a year in the community, his incarceration in a correctional institution reaches an average cost of $1,966 a year. Surprising, too, is the fact that rehabilitation is much more effective in a community than in a prison setting. Although misdemeanant correctional costs are somewhat lower ($142 in the community versus $1,146 in an institutional setting), they too show the rising economic problem. The need to develop localized but progressive juvenile and adult correctional programs is all the more apparent. Not only must probation and parole services be better integrated with prosecution and judicial systems, but they must be run with greater sensitivity and awareness of major gains in behavioral understanding.

Correctional Programs Are Needed

Public representatives, unwilling to revise prison correctional philosophy and operations, stymie rehabilitative efforts. Correctional educational and vocational training programs must be upgraded. Since more than one half of all adult inmates usually have not completed elementary school, the need to develop adequate elementary and secondary school facilities is apparent. College level courses, too, should be added to advance the competitive potential of the released inmate.

Progress here is severely hampered by lack of instructors. More than 6,000 scholastic, academic, and vocational teachers are currently needed in correctional institutions, while an additional 10,700 persons are required if an effective academic and vocational program is to be developed. Although vocational training is most adequately carried out in connection with present prison industries, more creative programs must be formulated. Business and organized labor must overcome their resistance to job retraining and institutional economic enterprise if men are to acquire adequate training and assume responsible positions. Current prison idleness must be replaced with productive retraining and renewal.

Short-term furloughs from penal institutions and work-release programs offer many opportunities to help overcome prison liabilities. Institutional home furloughs, used most extensively in Mississippi and Michigan, have been successful in more than 99 percent of all cases. Work release has been successful in nearly 85 percent of the cases. Under its provisions, prisoners pay for transportation, incidental expenses, clothing, tools, union fees, and income taxes from their daily earnings. Although some states may require the offender to participate in room-and-board costs, the remaining income may be sent to dependents, used to pay fines and previous debts, or saved for post-release expenses. The work-release program not only allows the offender to salvage his self-respect and to save money, but it also enables him to work productively at a job which may be useful in his future. When coordinated with special prerelease guidance programs, which encourage the step-by-step reentry of the offender into the community, community reentrance adjustments are minimized.

The President's Commission on Law Enforcement and Administration of Justice suggested that future correctional institutions be small and be located in or near cities from which they draw inmates. Designed for medium or minimal security offenders, the model institution should resemble a normal residential setting as much as possible. Not only should the rooms have no bars, but inmates should be encouraged to eat at small tables in an informal atmosphere. The institution should have classrooms, recreational facilities, day rooms, and a shop and library, but most educational and vocational training programs should be centered in the local community. This prototype, the Commission suggested, shifts the focus of corrections from temporary banishment of the offender to a revised process of combined control and treatment. If supported by flexible laws and policies, this arrangement would permit, according to the Commission, the use of institutional restraint to maximize long-range rehabilitative ends and would lessen the conflict between criminal offenders and judicial or correctional representatives.

Probation and Parole

The growing unwillingness to sentence minor offenders to prison has led to increased use of probation. Under most probation procedures, the offender remains in the community under the jurisdiction of a probation officer who supervises his future conduct for a designated period. From 60 to 90 percent of the probationers studied in 15 different surveys completed probation requirements without revocation. Somewhat sobering, however, is the fact that a third of the 250 counties studied in a national corrections survey provided no probation service. Release on suspended sentence without supervision or institutionalization were the only alternatives in these instances. When coupled with the fact that most minor offenders are released from local institutions or jails without parole, the inadequacies of modern corrections remain vivid. The failure to develop community resources and facilities to reduce juvenile delinquency and adult misdemeanors allows the continuation of deviance by social default. Overdependence on institutionalization as a means of social control lets the local community ignore its basic problem and obligation.

Approximately 6,100 new juvenile probation and parole officers are needed at the present time, if recommended case loads of 35 offenders per probation officer are to be realized. Under current delinquency and crime rates another 23,000 officers would be necessary by 1975 to maintain the same essential juvenile services. Adult felon probation and parole officers need to be tripled immediately, reaching a total of 23,000 by 1975. But the picture is even more grave on the misdemeanor level, where the greatest volume of criminal activity occurs. Only 1,944 officers are employed in comparison to the 15,400 currently needed. An estimated 22,000 probation and parole officers will be needed to screen and classify the more than 5 million persons who will be referred to the lower courts by 1975. The manpower demand far exceeds the supply.

Subprofessionals and Community Volunteers

One of the more creative recent developments in corrections has been the employment of subprofessionals and volunteers in community corrections. Subprofessionals, whether former inmates or persons without major training in social work or behavioral sciences, are often able to identify closely with a minor offender at a critical point in his life.

In Texas, for example, volunteers establish contact with parolees on release and help arrange jobs or secure readmission to school. Offering counsel and friendship, volunteers serve as successful friends who can offer the offender insight into the "other side" of life. The mere use of subprofessionals, however, cannot overcome the basic problems of parole and probation. Until local schools, plants, industries, medical facilities, religious organizations, and political agencies accept their share of community crime responsibility, marginal offenders will not be adequately aided. The delinquent, misdemeanant, or felon, already marginal, has too often been rejected by his own parents, educators, employers, and less criminal peers. When labeled delinquent or criminal, his alienation, frustration, and sense of hopelessness are formally confirmed. Institutional confinement only dramatizes the personal segregation already effected as the youth was shunted away from "good youngsters" so that he would not corrupt them.

The Reentry Problem

The problem of the reentry of delinquents into the mainstream of society both before and after institutionalization must be solved. The youth who is expelled from school needs reentry as much as the youth being released from the juvenile institution. Juvenile deviancy is too often indirectly encouraged by those who claim their dislike for antisocial behavior. As long as these persons ignore their responsibility in the creation of crime, delinquency, and social hopelessness, the issue will remain unsolved. Closer community coordination offers hope for the future rehabilitation of the offender. But as long as probation, parole, and volunteer workers direct their attention to the psychological character of the offender and fail to perceive that his psychological being is also a social creation, the issue of crime and delinquency will remain untouched. Future probation and parole officers must become the basic link between the offender and community institutions. They will have to mediate between the offender and the job or school which the delinquent may have rejected or which may have rejected him. Bridging the gap between the individual and the society, the future officer must interpret both to each other.

The formation of a community youth service bureau, designed to provide personal, social, psychological, or other services to the youth in his own community, must be encouraged. Although such a bureau would involve readjustments in probation and parole policy and juvenile-court philosophy and practice, it promises to be a more meaningful approach to juvenile rehabilitation. Since success in the community depends on community willingness to accept a known violator, effective rehabilitation can only be achieved by full cooperation of community institutions. A service purchase program, pioneered by the Vocational Rehabilitative Administration for handicapped persons, gives some insight into future potentials. Under its provisions, counselors are provided with funds which they can invest in psychological, vocational, educational, medical and other services for their clients as needed in order to effect their initial readjustment to the community upon release.

Other programs oriented to the delinquent and criminal population, including personal or group counseling, family therapy, special tutoring, and increased use of foster or group homes and occasional short-term confinement, have offered new techniques and procedures for future rehabilitation. Only by redirection of current correctional emphases and social attitudes can the individual be encouraged to redefine his behavior and seek new goals.

The Crux of the Problem

The vast number of delinquents are scared, love-lacking youth who are products of similar family relationships. They share some values and attitudes which differ from but are related to Christian moral concepts. Often they reject female domination of the home and seek manhood through overcompensation and self-exaggeration. They may reject Christian values as incompatible with the struggle for ghetto survival and seek a redefined religious concept which stabilizes their existence and gives meaning to their conception of personal and social reality.

7
Christian Witness and the Rehabilitation of Men

All men share a common humanity, though they may differ in personal skill, racial characteristics, status or individual wealth.

Sharing a common humanity, men also share a common tendency to criminality. What man in society has not been a delinquent? What woman not a "borrower" or thief? The student who plagiarizes, the juvenile who drinks, the youthful couple who share sexual favors in a parked car, the businessman who fails to report his full income, and the politician who accepts financial payment for legislative deals — all share in crime.

Church members too may be delinquents and criminals. Their very church membership and participation may exempt them from arrest or trial; they are known as respectable citizens in the community. Church members are normally law-abiding citizens, but some have fallen into theft, embezzlement, robbery, or even murder. The professing Christian, despite his intentions, often violates the law. Traffic, tax, and housing laws are often hedged or ignored.

The Christian Is Both Sinner and Saint

Although Christians have been regenerated and brought to faith in Christ by the power of the Holy Spirit, they remain sinners. By faith in Christ they are saints through the forgiveness of the Gospel, but they retain the weakness of a sinful nature. By faith Christians are forgiven and justified before God. They live in the knowledge that Jesus Christ has redeemed them from sin and its judgment by His life, death, and resurrection. Christians do not live in pride over their good actions, but in humility they confess their failures and by the power of God's Holy Spirit live in the assurance of God's grace through Christ. Living in this forgiveness-grace relationship with God, they have a loving and understanding attitude toward others. The love of Christ moves them to be quick to forgive and forget.

Christian love shows concern for violators, criminals, and those who work with them because they are people for whom Christ died. Christians living in grace will not be quick to denounce offenders, because all share a common humanity. The position of being sinners while saints by the grace of Christ will not permit them to be careless and indifferent toward rehabilitation of the criminal, education of the juvenile delinquent, and employment of the ex-convict.

The Christian, who depends on God's forgiveness, is unable to accept simple and easy "solutions" to lawbreaking and crime. Certain of his own faith and future, he spends his energy serving his human brother wherever he may be found. He makes no restrictions on age, sex, race, location, or type of crime committed. A Christian knows that every man has the inner struggle against his own evil nature. He knows that men are influenced by conditions in their social environment; he understands the demands and temptations of a bad neighborhood. He believes that his own new life in Christ is also intended to be a new life for others. Christ suffered and died for all men, including criminals and prisoners. Rather than dehumanize and degrade, the Christian attempts to elevate and help. In faith and hope that God may bless his efforts, the Christian moves forward to help find the answers to poverty, social hatred, individual fear, personal alienation, political graft, individual or group dehumanization, and delinquency or crime.

The Christian in Action

The Christian man is God's representative on earth. In gratitude for free and full salvation, he is called to live his life as an expression of Christ's love. As a sinner he is often tempted to become an instrument of the world and of selfish interests. The Spirit of God, working through Word and sacrament, renews his faith and calls him to action for the good of his neighbor and the glory of God.

The action of the Christian takes many forms. He works to better the social conditions which contribute to the crime increase. He promotes educational systems that prepare all men for an active life of employment and social cooperation. He strives to enhance the dignity of the dirty, the poor, the alienated, and the vulnerable. A Christian works to provide care for the juvenile, psychiatric treatment for the sex offender, and community acceptance of the violator making a new start. Interested in the quality and sensitivity of government to human need, he resists those politicians who accept bribes and kickbacks and share in other "acceptable" crimes in society. He seeks out the qualified, uncorrupted, and hopefully incorruptible to guarantee the best in political leadership.

Christians also seek to promote just use of police and court power through the improvement of legal education and law enforcement. Working to bring the best available knowledge of human behavior to the attention of legislative leaders and the public, Christians are catalysts for improvement. In sincere concern for unpopular causes like alcoholism and narcotic addiction, they assume responsibility for victim rehabilitation. The Christian man feels the responsibility to do whatever is necessary to improve public or home conditions, educational systems, or community facilities. He demands reasonable and needed government programs and is willing to assume the obligation of higher taxes for value received. His perspective is communitywide. His responsibility is to God and his fellowman. Loving his neighbor because of Christ, he works for the public welfare. He is one to whom much has been given. From him much is also expected.

The Christian and Penal Reform

The results of the present penal system can no longer be acceptable to Christians who recognize that prisons have often become places of social contamination. Prison homosexuality, idleness, overcrowding, and excessively long sentences, sometimes for misdeeds not requiring imprisonment, serve to demoralize the prisoner, reinforce his criminal behavior, and minimize his future social usefulness.

Christians should assume the leadership in pressing for prison reform and in demanding that local jails and misdemeanant institutions be integrated into coherent and vital state correctional programs. By serving as the conscience of the community, Christians have the opportunity to lead political leaders to a new awareness of problems and of the need for better treatment and facilities.

The Focus Must Be Larger than the Prison

The Christian focus cannot be limited to facilities and programs; released offenders need to be reintegrated into the community. Other offenders can be more effectively treated through the use of local resources than by imprisonment. While maximum security offenders may be effectively contained in a congregate prison distant from their home communities, the vast number of offenders are better treated through the coordinated use of community resources designed to overcome the deficiencies evidenced in the delinquent-criminal situation. Institutionalization of young men (and women) in congregate prisons which are dissimilar from the communities to which they will ultimately return does nothing to solve the reintegration problem. The need to identify and coordinate community resources, whether in the form of jobs in industry, psychological-psychiatric counseling services, physical treatment facilities, or other pertinent outlets are central to a local offender reintegration program. Christians can serve to mobilize community leadership and can work in cooperation with the courts and probation-parole officials to develop a coherent and comprehensive local treatment setting.

The Potential of Probation and Parole

The systems of probation and parole offer the Christian good opportunities to assist in the work of rehabilitation. Actual supervision often consists of nothing more than a 10- to 15-minute interview once or twice a month and superficial counseling as the need arises. Probation and parole officers, plagued by large work loads, too often supervise the individual from a distance rather than provide professional aid to the person who is attempting to readjust to the community situation.

Since approximately 95 percent of all offenders will ultimately return to the community, Christians have a special interest in treatment and rehabilitation, probation and parole.

The Christian realizes that purging the community of the wrongdoer does little to guarantee community security when the wrongdoer returns at a later time without adequate change in personal goals. Convicted men are the forgotten men of the technological civilization. Forgotten before their conviction, they remain forgotten in the correctional institution and their community.

The church has not entirely forgotten these men. Protestant and Catholic chaplains have been placed in many penal institutions. Church volunteers have assisted in helping the former prisoners adjust to life. But much of the church's energy is directed to the normal and healthy segment of the population. Some of the greatest needs are found in those who are in prison or are unwanted because of a prison record. Until all Christian people view the delinquent and the criminal as their brothers, they will generally remain insensitive to those who have little hope and are alienated from the predominant political, economic, and social systems.

Am I the Problem or the Solution?

Christians need to ask, "Am I part of the problem of delinquency and crime, or am I part of the solution process?" When church people oppose decent schools, adequate homes, and valid employment opportunities because of racial fears, political ideology, unenlightened religious views, or opposition to higher taxes, they only aggravate the problem which they claim they solve.

Christians who thank God for His blessings in

a rich and favored land cannot be content with the wastes of personnel and property which delinquency, crime, and imprisonment bring. Their love for people constrains them to find new channels and define new structures for the needs of men. The Christian is no longer willing to measure the prevention of delinquency and crime in terms of dollar costs. He sees man as he is and Christ's vision of what he may become. The Christian remembers: "There, but for the grace of God, go I." And he remembers that his neighbor is everyone who is in need of his love.

Questions for Discussion

1. In what areas may the general public help solve the crime problem?
2. In what ways does the definition of crime affect the amount of crimes committed?
3. Why do the "myths" persist in the face of evidence to the contrary?
4. Do you agree that ideas of what is crime may vary from one group to another, or should there be some things that are always right or wrong? What are these things?
5. Of the various theories as to the origins of criminality, which ones reflect Christian attitudes?
6. Can you describe other ways in which upper- or middle-class persons may commit undetected crimes in business practices?
7. In what way does the public desire for sensational news affect the issue of free press and fair trial? Is the public interest greater than the private interest?
8. What do you know of the juvenile court process and handling of juveniles in your community? (An investigation may be worthwhile.)
9. Are the courts "handcuffing" the police by their recent decisions? What are the facts?
10. What type of training is available for the enforcement agencies in your community? Is this adequate?
11. What are the minimum and maximum salaries for enforcement officers in your community? What qualifications are necessary for initial employment and advancement? What is the turnover rate?

12. In what ways can a congregation encourage better enforcement procedures?
13. How can the church aid in the rehabilitation of offenders: adult and juvenile?
14. Is the prison an effective institution? What problems does it cause? What benefits does it render?
15. How can a criminal be reached? Is simple preaching enough?
16. What are your own attitudes toward delinquency? toward criminality?

For Further Reading

Federal Bureau of Investigation. *The Uniform Crime Reports*. Washington, D. C.: U. S. Government Printing Office, 1967.

Lunden, Walter A. *Crimes and Criminals*. Ames: Iowa State University Press, 1967.

President's Commission on Law Enforcement and Administration of Justice. *The Challenge of Crime in a Free Society*. Washington, D. C.: U. S. Government Printing Office, 1967.

Sykes, Gresham. *A Society of Captives*. New York: Atheneum, 1965.

Report of the Presidential Commission on Civil Disorders. New York: Bantam Book, 1968.

Walker, Nigel. *Crime and Punishment in Britain*. Chicago: Aldine Publishing Co., 1966.

A general view of The Criminal Justice System

This chart seeks to present a simple yet comprehensive view of the movement of cases through the criminal justice system. Procedures in individual jurisdictions may vary from the pattern shown here. The differing weights of line indicate the relative volumes of cases disposed of at various points in the system, but this is only suggestive since no nationwide data of this sort exists.

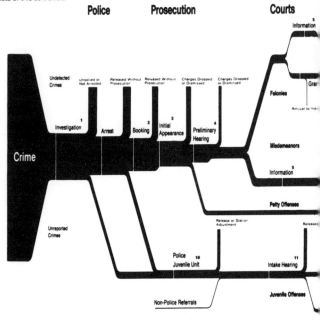

Police　　**Prosecution**　　**Courts**

- Information
- Undetected Crimes
- Unsolved or Not Arrested
- Released Without Prosecution
- Released Without Prosecution
- Charges Dropped or Dismissed
- Charges Dropped or Dismissed
- Grand
- Felonies
- Refusal to Indict
- 1 Investigation
- Arrest
- 2 Booking
- 3 Initial Appearance
- Preliminary Hearing 4
- Crime
- Misdemeanors
- 5 Information
- Petty Offenses
- Unreported Crimes
- Release or Station Adjustment
- Released
- Police Juvenile Unit 10
- Intake Hearing 11
- Juvenile Offenses
- Non-Police Referrals

1 May continue until trial.

2 Administrative record of arrest. First step at which temporary release on bail may be available.

3 Before magistrate, commissioner, or justice of peace. Formal notice of charge, advice of rights. Bail set. Summary trials for petty offenses usually conducted here without further processing.

4 Preliminary testing of evidence against defendant. Charge may be reduced. No separate preliminary hearing for misdemeanors in some systems.

5 Charge filed by prosecutor on basis of information submitted by police or citizens. Alternative to grand jury indictment; often used in felonies, almost always in misdemeanors.

6 Reviews whether Government evidence sufficient to justify trial. Some States have no grand jury system; others seldom use it.

Corrections

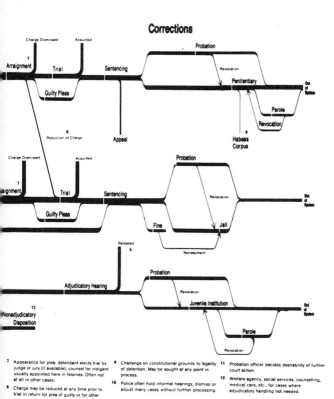

7 Appearance for plea; defendant elects trial by judge or jury (if available); counsel for indigent usually appointed here in felonies. Often not at all in other cases.

8 Charge may be reduced at any time prior to trial in return for plea of guilty or for other reasons.

9 Challenge on constitutional grounds to legality of detention. May be sought at any point in process.

10 Police often hold informal hearings, dismiss or adjust many cases without further processing.

11 Probation officer decides desirability of further court action.

12 Welfare agency, social services, counselling, medical care, etc., for cases where adjudicatory handling not needed.

125